blue
rider
press

I See You
Made an Effort

ALSO BY ANNABELLE GURWITCH

You Say Tomato, I Say Shut Up
with Jeff Kahn

Fired! Tales of the Canned, Canceled,
Downsized, & Dismissed

BLUE RIDER PRESS · A MEMBER OF PENGUIN GROUP (USA) · NEW YORK

I See You
Made an Effort

COMPLIMENTS,

INDIGNITIES, AND

SURVIVAL STORIES

FROM THE EDGE OF

50

Annabelle Gurwitch

blue
rider
press

Published by the Penguin Group
Penguin Group (USA) LLC
375 Hudson Street
New York, New York 10014

USA · Canada · UK · Ireland · Australia
New Zealand · India · South Africa · China

penguin.com
A Penguin Random House Company

Library of Congress Cataloging-in-Publication Data

Gurwitch, Annabelle.
I see you made an effort : compliments, indignities, and survival
stories from the edge of fifty / Annabelle Gurwitch.
p.   cm.
Includes bibliographical references and index.
ISBN 978-0-399-16618-1
1. Aging—Humor.   2. Middle-aged women—Humor.   I. Title.
PN6231.A43G87   2014   2013037792
814'.54—dc23

Printed in the United States of America
1   3   5   7   9   10   8   6   4   2

BOOK DESIGN BY MEIGHAN CAVANAUGH

For my big sister, Lisa,

thanks for saving me a seat at the table

Contents

I See You
Made an Effort

STAY FUNNY

On the day I turned forty-nine the first solicitation from AARP appeared in my email in-box. At a glance, I thought it might be an ad for white-collar prison uniforms. A couple is pictured dressed in matching cotton pastel sweaters and pleated Dockers. The entire outfit screams, *Here, take my libido and hold it for the rest of my life, which won't last much longer anyway.* The man has his arms encircling the woman's waist. Is he propping her up because she's suffering from osteoporosis, or helpfully disguising her muffin top? The expressions on their faces can only be described as resigned.

The AARP offers you a refrigerated travel bag when you join. What's the refrigerated part for? Medications, no doubt. Medications that require refrigeration? They're not fooling around. Perhaps I'll consider joining when they feature couples in matching

Jil Sander elegance and offer a gym bag or a Shiraz of the Month club membership. Just something that doesn't advertise *Your health is your top concern while traveling.* For the record, it is. I was just diagnosed as prediabetic but I don't need my luggage to remind me.

Something had to give.

Things that had seemed solid were falling away. My attitude, my family, my future and my face, everything had lost its shape.

The mothers I had grown up with were disappearing before my eyes. My own mom was diagnosed with breast cancer, and with Bonnie Franklin and Jean Stapleton gone, I started checking up on Florence Henderson's health. All of the Ramones had left the building except for the ones you never cared about to begin with.

My son wasn't speaking to me. I was unemployed and my parents urgently needed to sell my childhood home. Should I go back to college, adopt another kid, get divorced, raise llamas? I couldn't afford a vacation so I was taking a lot of naps.

I tried keeping gratitude lists, stronger vibrators, cheap massages and better moisturizers. I tried praying to a God I didn't even believe in.

When I began contemplating having *Under New Management* inked just below my C-section scar, I made an appointment with my gynecologist.

As I left his office with my stack of prescriptions for hormone replacement therapy gels, patches and pills, he held his hand up to wave good-bye. "Stay . . ." Pause. It was a big pause, though there are definitely no pregnant pauses in my life anymore. Stay what? What would he say? Would it be that adage girls signed yearbooks with at my junior high school, "Stay the same, never change"? Stay healthy? Stay happy? Stay hydrated? Would he go all Bob Dylan on me, "Stay forever young"? Nope.

"Stay . . . funny," he said.

Forty is the new thirty? I've heard that many times and I've said it just as often. Interestingly, the saying "Fifty is the new forty" has never really caught on because it's not. Fifty is still fifty.

Fucking fifty.

AUTUMN LEAVES

> **Dear God,**
>
> **Please let me still be fuckable at fifty.**

My computer was moving sluggishly. A year ago, upon pressing the start button, my machine swiftly jumped to attention.
Now the familiar sight of documents dotting the photograph
of my thirteen-year-old son was replaced by a black bar inch-
ing across a dull gray expanse, like an octogenarian with a walker
creeping through an intersection. Then the software failed to
load altogether. It was going to take a stroke of genius to get it
working again.

The Glendale Galleria Apple Store is staffed by a crew whose
average age could be summed up as: if you have to ask, you're too
old to want to hear the answer. After checking in, I am told my
personal genius will meet me at the Bar.* *Homo genius* are outfit-

---

*Word on the street is Apple wants to hire more women, but go to your local store,
and you'll notice that the majority of the Geniuses are male.

ted uniformly in T-shirts announcing their membership in an elite tech-savvy species. Mine sports a headband, which artfully musses his hair. He is wearing a name tag that reads "AuDum." I ask him how he pronounces it.

"Is it a creative spelling of the first man, Adam? Is it a Sanskrit chant—Auuuduuuum? A percussive sound?"

"No," he replies. "It's pronounced *autumn*, like the season."

"Are you in a band?"

"No, my mother gave me that name."

"You belong to a generation of great names," I tell him. I am thinking of the kids whose instruments I check out every Friday afternoon in the music department at my son's school. Each student's name is more interesting than the next: Lilit, Anush, Reason, Butterfly, Summer and Summer Butterfly, which seems like both a name and a tone poem. I make sure to repeat their names before wishing them a good weekend, reasoning that in classes of forty-five students, this might be the only moment in their school day when they get individually recognized. Or maybe I'm doing it because it's just fun to recite their names out loud. Coming as I do from a generation of Mandys and Mindys, Lisas and Leslies, AuDum's name is an instant clue that my Genius and I are separated by decades in which progenitors have gifted their offspring with intriguing names.

AuDum begins talking about his mother and I hold my breath, wondering if he will say that she is my age. Thankfully, he says she's a bit older, sixty-two. She's a speech pathologist who lives in Albuquerque and he admires her work. I am charmed by his obvious affection for his mother. He has been well cared for, I think,

. . . . . .

as I notice that he has good teeth. Braces? Maybe not, but definitely regular dental care. As he examines my computer, he tells me my hard drive is dying.

"But it's so young—it's only a few years old."

He explains that computer years are like dog years times three, making my computer only slightly younger than I am.

"But there were no outward signs. It was doing just fine until recently."

"Nobody knows exactly why computers fail," he tells me. "It's not like people, who have a steady decline—the end can come without warning. You're catching it just in time," he says, adding, "do you have an external hard drive?" I tell him I do, thinking that if my Apple Time Machine* weren't the size of a wallet I would jump inside it and go back in time so I could be his age. While I was there, I would also correct a few of the numerous errors in judgment I've made in my almost fifty years on the planet.

To start with, I would change all my PIN numbers, secret passwords, and security codes to the exact same thing.† I also went door-to-door to register voters for John Kerry in 2004, made phone calls for John Edwards in 2000, and took pottery classes after the maudlin melodrama *Ghost*, with Demi Moore and Patrick Swayze, came out in 1990. I'm not sure which was the biggest

---

*The Apple Time Capsule, or Time Machine, is the most technically advanced and popular external hard-drive gadget Apple has on the market. I bought it because I liked the name.

†I would try to come up with one memorable code but not: 123456, 12345678, or Password, Pussy, or Baseball. A successful hack of millions of Yahoo accounts on July 12, 2012, revealed that's what the majority of people use as passwords.

. . . . . .

misstep, but a trip back in time could, at the very least, keep half a dozen ill-formed ashtrays out of California landfills.

Judging from his appearance, it seems a distinct and sobering possibility that AuDum Genius might have been born the same year I was throwing clay.

"So, how old are you?"

"Twenty-six."

He is closer in age to my son than me by a decade. As he checks out my computer, I pepper him with questions. "What qualifies one to be a Genius? Is there much training? An IQ test?"

Just as he's about to answer, another of his tribe, Sean Genius, comes over and deferentially asks what even I know to be a simple question. "What do you do if someone forgets her iTunes password?" AuDum helps him out and I compliment him by noting that some Geniuses seem more gifted than others. He tells me that he was certified at the thirty-two-acre Apple campus, located at 1 Infinite Loop in Cupertino, California. The hotels are owned by Apple, the blankets have an Apple stamp, and would-be Geniuses eat on plates stamped with the Apple logo in Apple-owned cafés and are regularly whisked past restricted areas where classified research takes place. In fact, he will return for further training soon.

"Ooh," I tease him excitedly. "You could be a spy, pretending you're there to train, but you're really sneaking in to collect intel for Intel. The James Bond of computer tech."

He looks at me blankly. Clearly the reference to Bond doesn't hold the kind of cachet it did for generations of men before him.

Should have said Jason Bourne. That's when he suggests a radical move.

"Are you up for it?"

"I am."

He wants to strip my computer down completely and then carefully, slowly and deliberately, he will reload my hard drive. In order to make this work, I will have to agree to do everything he says, even if it sounds a bit unusual.

"In order to give something, we have to take something away," he tells me. Is he quoting the Bible or a sacred Steve Jobsian aphorism? I have no idea, but he had me at "reload."

We will need to download any applications I use and the process may take all night. During that time, I shouldn't do anything to harm or disturb the computer, he warns, or we'll have to start all over again and can I manage that kind of painstaking process? I'm forty-nine years old, I have all of my own teeth, most of my wedding china is still intact, and the baby who was cut out of my abdomen while I was awake has made it to puberty under my watch, so yes, I think I can do that. I nod my assent, swallowing hard. He tells me to take everything off.

I remove my data silently and swiftly. He begins his maneuvers, and I want to hear more about his mother.

"Were you always close, or did you find your way back to her as an adult?"

"Oh, we were on the same team until maybe thirteen or fourteen and then it got tough. She was having a hard time, too. She got divorced, changed careers, we moved around, but

. . . . . .

then things turned around after I went to college. Now we're close."

I take out a pen and paper to write his words down—like I'm an anthropologist taking field notes on the maturation process of young men. His grandmother died last month and his mother is "freaked" about being the oldest person left in her family. He's been calling a lot to help her make peace with that.

His hands are nice, I notice, nails filed, but a quick glance down the counter shows me that all Geniuses have clean hands and filed nails. Maybe it's code, like the way Disney once required employees at the park to be clean-shaven.* I may be looking at the last of the Apple manicures, but I hope not. It's nice to see good grooming on twenty-somethings. It's kind of old-school, or rather, my school.

His hands glide confidently over my keyboard, but my laptop keeps stalling so I have to keep reentering my password. I try to punch in the digits breezily, but he's standing so close, right next to my crooked pinky, the one with osteoarthritis. The process is laborious as I attempt to type with my pinky tucked under my palm, hoping he doesn't notice the swollen middle joint. It's possible, even probable, for someone so young to assume it's broken or disfigured from a sports injury—at least I hope so. My Genius sets the download in motion, hands me my computer, and with a brief good-bye, he promises that we'll finish what we started in

---

*In January 2012, under pressure from Disneyland Paris park employees who insisted on keeping their goatees, Disney gave up its no-facial-hair policy.

. . . . . .

the morning. I exit, cradling my computer through the mall, into my car, and back home.

I am an impatient person. I've never managed to carry out complicated recipes or blow-dry my hair all the way to the back of my head, but I am on a mission, and when I arrive home I leave the computer to complete the process. I instruct both my husband and son not to disturb it under any circumstances.

That night, everything I do seems supercharged with new purpose.

The next morning, after driving my son to school, I shower and stand in my closet, wondering what to wear. I have no idea. I haven't known what to put on for the last few years. I'm aging out of my wardrobe.

Skirts are too short. The legs are still good, but the folds of skin at the knee should not be seen, unless in colored tights, but even then, colored tights just don't seem age-appropriate. Many of my dresses are just too flouncy, ruffles circling the face are too Humpty Dumpty, flared skirts too flirty, tight clothing looks lumpy and anything blousy seems to emphasize my lack of a waist. Is this the moment I head into the Eileen Fisher years?

In my thirties, I glanced at Fisher's ads with fleeting interest, but as I edged into my forties, I began to linger on the images. Even with a cursory look, Eileen Fisher's clothes look like a cross between a hospital gown and a toga. What is the message? We need soft fabrics next to our dried-out skin—anything with more texture might chafe? We must disguise our bodies in flowing robes lest we appear overtly sexual—or worse, turn others off?

. . . . . .

Eileen shows only solid colors, no patterns at all, ever, as if to suggest that patterns might clash with the lines and angles on our faces. I do seem to look better in solid colors, and though the hospital togas threaten to reduce us to clichéd depictions of elder counsels in dystopian science fiction movies, Fisher's draping fabrics do smooth out some of the indignities of aging. Swaths of material gently cascading over the area where your waistline once was can make you appear . . . if not slimmer, then longer. Leaving your house wearing a duvet cover could probably work, too. Ironically, Fisher uses young models in her ads now. Her website has just one gray-haired lady, and she isn't even modeling the clothes*—she's featured in a video tutorial on how to tie a scarf. The other clothing lines that cater to women over forty are Chico's, with their loud resort patterns and animal prints, and Jil Sander, whose minimalistic designs and color palette (ranging from gray to charcoal) are subtle and chic but so expensive I can't even afford to gaze upon them. The only thing I've found that fits both my body and state of mind is business suits, but I can't show up for my Genius appointment dressed like I'm headed to a corporate board meeting.

I try on a pair of new jeans that I was steered to purchase by a mother of four who's in her fifties. My friend likes them because they have a high waist without being mom-jeans boxy. I pair them with a dark blue button-down shirt and a black sweater. I look

---

*In 2009, when Eileen Fisher announced she wanted to target younger customers, a lot of women over fifty were pissed off! Incidentally, American women over fifty spend more than $25 billion a year on clothes. We also have more discretionary income than any other demographic group. Why'd you break up with us, Eileen?

. . . . . .

like a plainclothes detective. It's the best I can do. I put on a minimal amount of makeup. Have to keep it light; at forty-nine, any excess looks like Sylvia Miles's aging hooker character from *Midnight Cowboy*. (It's worth noting that Ms. Miles was actually thirty-seven when she shot that film.)

Then, I carefully twist a length of bright yellow silk into "The Pretzel." Yes, I did watch the six-and-a-half-minute scarf-tying video on the Fisher site. A middle-aged woman dressed in a simple black outfit, no jewelry, with a close-cropped hairstyle I call the "man-do" (a look favored by Judi Dench, elderly nuns, and white-pride militias), solemnly wraps herself in colored scarves, smiling wanly each time she completes a knot. Over and over and over again. Some techniques are genuinely intriguing, but I was also tempted to lob the "Loop and Drape" over a ceiling lamp before roping it around my neck and stepping off a chair. The scarf's official purpose, like that of its older cousin, the turtleneck, is to cover the gobbler, but standing in my closet, I realize that the scarf also adds color and some je ne sais quoi. I know what the "quoi" is now—it's the last vestige of feminine flair of the pared-down wardrobe of the middle-aged woman. I cast it aside and leave the house looking like a cop.

I arrive at the store and start to panic. I don't see my Genius anywhere and I fear he has taken my computer through some kind of unconventional protocol and it will never be the same. But then I catch his eye as he emerges from behind an Apple paneled door and I break into a sweat. Is it a hot flash? *Oh, God.* But no, it's something else. I have fallen in love with AuDum Genius. The story of his affection for his mother, coupled with my being totally dependent on whoever can repair what has become my most essential appendage, has endeared him to me.* He smiles and I can see he's wearing that same headband and his hair might be a little greasy, but his nails are filed and the teeth are good. The teeth are good, I assure myself. I can live with that.

I'm not on the appointment list projected on the Apple screen, but he motions me over to the Genius Bar. I stride ahead, pushing through the pain from a recent tennis injury so my limp will go unnoticed. ("Recent" meaning five years ago, when I twisted my right ankle playing tennis and the orthopedist told me I had "boomeritis."†) I sit attentively as AuDum resuscitates my hard drive and reveals more about himself. It is our second date, after all. He studied urban planning. He likes to sketch and takes on small graphic-design gigs because there's a dearth of work in his field. He shares an apartment with two roommates and he is thinking of going to Norway, where there might be better employment opportunities.

"You should do that. It's the perfect time in your life to have an adventure. If it doesn't work out, you can chalk it up to 'things I did in my twenties,'" I tell him, his head buried in my device. "I have twenty-three years of experience on you, so I know what I'm talking about," I add with authority. I have now announced

---

*In February 2012, iVillage published a survey indicating two-thirds of married women prefer Facebooking to sucking face, or any other sucking, for that matter.
†"Boomeritis" is an officially recognized medical term coined by an orthopedic surgeon in 1999 for injuries boomer-aged people get when they exercise as vigorously as when they were younger. I spent six months in "the boot." The boot has become something of a status symbol, a middle-age must-have accessory—it's an advertisement of your virility.

my age. He's a Genius, so he might have figured it out already, but he doesn't say, "You look young for your age," which I decide to let pass without comment, even though I have read that Geniuses are supposed to make the customers feel warm and welcome in the store and that would be the warmest and most welcome thing to say.

He's typing in codes and waxing on about which cities have the best infrastructures and I am fantasizing about his possible Wikipedia entry: *After AuDum Genius met Annabelle Gurwitch* [we have the same initials—we can share monogrammed luggage and towels], *he began his innovative and transformative design work.* But I know that's a stretch. I don't have the money to become his patron. I would love to be his Peggy Guggenheim; alas, the best I can aim for is to be his Mrs. Robinson.*

This idea has nothing to do with my actual marriage, though I have started to suspect that the timbre of my husband's burp has been specifically calibrated to annoy me. More than half of our communication revolves around who will volunteer first to pick up our kid, our dinner, or our sex life. If you were to catch a glimpse of my face during the throes of passion, you might mistake my expression for that of a bartender at four a.m., shaking her last martini—one who enjoys her work and wants to please every customer, but is also relieved her shift is ending soon.

All of which is to say that we're in the middle of our marriage. I have come to appreciate that there are some great things about

---

*It's been widely noted, but is always worth repeating, that Anne Bancroft was only six years Dustin Hoffman's senior when she played his seductress in *The Graduate.*

. . . . . .

the middle of a marriage. The way neither of us understands fla-vored coffees or movies where people exchange bodies, and no matter how angry we are, we'll stop in the middle of an argu-ment to watch our cats do something cute. But middles can be thankless. Beginnings are always exciting, even if in a car-crash/impending-disaster way. Endings, even heart-wrenching ones, can be energizing. Friends who have gotten divorced go on diets and dates. Even when those end badly they make for good stories.

The historical precedent for the kind of female May-December fling I'm considering isn't great, especially if you're looking for something long-term. In fiction, it doesn't end well for Emma Bovary, Countess Olenska, or Mrs. Robinson, for that matter. Even Samantha's infamously tireless libido in *Sex and the City* couldn't forestall the inevitable breakup with her hunky blond boy toy Smith.

I also hate the term "cougar." There isn't a name for men who date younger women; it's just considered normal. I do have girl-friends who have booty calls with younger men, and one friend who, after two divorces and three children, is happily dating a woman ten years younger. Another, also divorced with kids, leads sex tours of Paris for women who, as she advertises on her website, have already "married, divorced, cut our hair off, and reinvented." All of that sounds positively exhausting to me. I had plenty of random sex in my twenties and thirties.

I have held a special fantasy for one of my exes. He's the path not taken. A tall, remote, Italian Catholic heartbreaker, the polar opposite of my five-six, adoring Jewish husband. That he dumped me unceremoniously, by all accounts is happily married with kids

. . . . . .

and has never once in twenty years reached out to me hasn't stopped me from daydreaming about the call or email imploring me to run away with him. That is, until I ran into him in a restaurant this year. He looked weathered but still had his rakish swagger. We embraced, but before the shock of this reunion could even register as sexual tension, he began recounting the details of his recent hip-replacement surgery.

Dear God, I just want one night of Genius sex before I hit the half-century mark.

But where would we do it? At his apartment? No. There might be hairs of unknown provenance on the soap, black towels, and sheets that haven't been changed recently. Plus, one of his roommates might be there, and no one can witness this act.

My house? No. What if he accidentally puts on one of my kid's T-shirts, strewn around the house as they are? We also have kid artwork hanging everywhere and it just seems wrong that we would sneak by the watercolor rendering of a dinosaur pooping as we head into the bedroom. On top of that, my menopausal brain fog makes it impossible to keep schedules straight, so there is a good chance I would pick an inopportune moment to hook up and AuDum would arrive just in time to witness our nightly ritual of haggling with our teenager over homework versus Internet time. But there's another big problem, and that's the "ick" factor of having sex in the bed I share with my husband. That didn't seem to bother California's governor Arnold Schwarzenegger when he had an affair with his housekeeper, whom he probably asked to make said bed afterward. Plus, at any given moment, a pair of Spanx might be crumpled in a ball at the foot

. . . . . .

of our bed, a tube of hormone replacement cream on the night-stand, or one of the many pairs of tweezers I hide around the house might have migrated under a pillow. Our bedroom is a minefield of erection killers—just ask my husband.

Cannot go to a cheap hotel. A cheap hotel does not figure into this or any other fantasy I have at this age. It will need to be pricey. I really can't afford an expensive destination, but it's the only way. Yes, I'll need to dip into our savings. Hopefully, I can write it off as a business expense, which it technically is. The business of getting old. Once I find the correct establishment, I'll go up to the room first, and AuDum will need to wait for a brief interval to avoid being spotted by anyone I know. This will give me time to get ready, and I need it.

It's been eighteen years since I've taken my clothes off in front of anyone other than my husband, my gynecologist and women in the locker room at the gym. I'll really need two or three weeks, if not months, to get my body affair-ready. I will also need to purchase new undergarments. I own bras and panties that are nice enough for fifteen years of marriage, but fall under the category of "underwear," and for an affair it will really need to be "lingerie." Plus, I will need to get the full Brazilian, which I tried once when I was pregnant but it was so painful, I left it half done. My single friends tell me that bare is the new black for men, so I hope the computer gets repaired quickly, as I will need to start acclimating myself to the hairless penis through pornographic Internet surfing.

What will AuDum Genius and I talk about? Best not to let it slip how pissed off I am that my son is getting a C in PE and that

. . . . . .

18

he's definitely not going to Ming-Na Davydov's bat mitzvah if he keeps it up. Or that I need to get a mole that's changed shape checked on a part of my back that I can't see, and would he check it? Safe topics might include movies or books, but not films about senior citizens falling in love at resorts in India, or anything with Meryl Streep, and no mentioning that I am currently reading a book titled *Why Men Die First*. I could suggest a late-night supper from room service, but he'd have to read the menu to me or I'd be pulling out my reading glasses. Note to self: Don't say, "In my day" out loud. Also avoid "nowadays." "Nowadays" is a touchstone used by aging persons to describe things that happened "in my day." The word "touchstone" is also a touchstone for AARP territory. Talking is out. Drinking is better.

While I wait for him, I'll put on mood music. Since he's about the same age as my nephews, I should put on some dubstep, only I hate its incessant thumping sound. I'm sure it sounds good if you're sucking on an Ecstasy pacifier at a rave in the desert, but I would rather have my spleen removed and filleted in front of me than be high in the middle of a sweaty crowd ringed by porta-potties. But if I put on something like Fleetwood Mac or, God forbid, Marvin Gaye, I risk dating myself. I've got it: *jazz*. Jazz has always been the perfect soundtrack for doing stupid things. But my son and his middle school band play all the standards, so jazz is off-limits.

A more pressing issue is, what's the right position? I'm not comfortable with someone ogling my ass if I can't observe the reaction, so doggie gets a thumbs-down. Missionary seems too same-old, same-old. It has to be something where I can achieve

. . . . . .

maximum attractiveness and get the most bang for my buck, so there's really only one choice. Movie sex. Up against a wall. *Glamour* magazine calls it "Stand and Deliver," while in the Kama Sutra it's "Climbing the Tree."

He leans into me, pressing my back hard up against the hotel wall. I tilt my face slightly upward, always a flattering angle, while his tongue traces the arc of my neck. The wall can be the perfect excuse for not completely disrobing; in fact, a wrap dress would be ideal, providing easy access while covering my posterior. He pushes the layers of my dress open and moves his hand up my thigh. I order him to take my panties off slowly so, as he kneels down, I'll have time to reach for the small tube of vaginal lubricant I've hidden in the folds of the wrap dress and quickly insert a dollop. Balancing on my good ankle, I wrap my leg around his body as I reach for him, but I've forgotten about a condom. We could take the half-hour AIDS test and forgo it, because there's no way I can get pregnant, but he can't know that; it would take away an element of danger, so I hope he's got one or the hotel can send one up quickly.

The only thing is, it's really tough to get the up-against-the-wall thing to work—our heights have to be just right, and he'll need a certain amount of upper-body strength, which he might not have developed working at the Apple store. I'll also need to keep my right leg aloft. If I can find a hotel room that has a rock-climbing wall—we are in Los Angeles, after all—I could anchor myself on a foothold. Yes! I wedge my heel into a foothold a few feet off the ground and pull him inside me.

"You're good to go."

. . . . . .

"Yes," I whisper. "I mean, yes?"

His voice is louder than I expected. I look down and see that I'm gripping the counter tightly. My mouth feels dry and my heart is pounding when something soft brushes my arm. It's a strand of hair. I snap my head to the right and see a girl with long straight brown hair. She is standing next to me at the counter. She's dressed in typical California fashion: sneakers, tight gym pants, and hoodie. She's a bit fleshy. She might even be pregnant. Her face is unmistakably young and fresh. Her skin is tan, tight, and creamy. She smells fertile.

"My next customer is here," he says, rotating my computer so I can see the folder he's created for my retrieved documents. He has named it "Old Annabelle."

"What?"

"Listen, if you need anything else," he says as he motions to another Genius, "Logan can take care of you."

"But, but . . ."

He points to the Apple screen and then to the luscious girl. "I've got to move on."

It falls to Logan Genius to move the items from the "Old Annabelle" folder into a new one that I've suggested we name "Vintage Annabelle." With a swift click, the offending word disappears. I am careful not to engage Logan in any small talk.

As Logan wraps up with tips on how to keep my computer as good as new, I catch sight of AuDum heading toward the exit. His shift must be over. The Apple shirt is gone, a nondescript T-shirt in its place. Out of his uniform, he looks different. His pants taper down his calves and stop just above his ankles in a

. . . . . .

way I find unflattering on someone past puberty. He has a slight lilt to his gait, as if his feet aren't solidly touching the ground. He gives me a little wave. It has a slightly reluctant quality to it. AuDum has sorted the clutter on my desktop, skimmed my documents and scanned through my most private emails. He knows everything about me there is to know without being intimate, but I can tell by the wave and his red high-top Keds that we will not be hooking up. AuDum leaves. I feel a bit sad but also extremely relieved.

AuDum goes home, heats up some ramen and takes out his sketchbook. He lies on his bed and starts to draw a woman. It's a woman with brown hair. The brunette in the hoodie. He's captured her inner glow. I have also made the picture. The side of my head hugs the corner of the frame, just out of focus. They will meet tonight for a drink. If that goes well, in two weeks they'll be at a rave, dancing to dubstep, somewhere in the desert. I hope they don't go and fall in love. After all, she might be pregnant and he really should move to Norway.

"Since you went away the days grow long, and soon I'll hear old winter's song." I hear the sound of the walking jazz bass line coming from my son's room. *"But I miss you most of all, my darling, when autumn leaves start to fall."*

WHEN BROWN WAS GOING TO BE THE NEW BLACK

> **Dear God,**
>
> **Please don't let me blow my entire 401(k) on expensive moisturizers.**

I've gotten dressed up. Dressed up to walk into a store.

I've assembled my most fashionable outfit to ensure that I will be treated with deference by people who are being paid to take my money. I'm wearing one of my corporate board meeting ensembles: a pinstriped wool skirt in chocolate, paired with a coffee-colored cashmere sweater. I purchased these investment pieces back when brown was going to be the new black and money was lubricated, back before everyone in America was vying for minimum-wage jobs just to stay underemployed. Two holes in the sweater are located at the waist, a small conciliatory gesture, perhaps, from the closet moths that are waging a war against my wardrobe. I have cleverly placed a belt over the offending area and am striding past the alluring displays of expensively packaged products hoping that the Krazy-Glued soles of my decade-old Miu Mius will hold for the brief amount of time it will take to run this errand. I have an entrance and exit strategy planned. It will be surgical, just like the U.S. involvement in Afghanistan.

I've come for a concealer. I've written down the manufacturer, product name and number so I don't make a mistake and purchase the incorrect shade. This product not only promises to restore the under-eye area to a refreshing brightness, but dotted across my chin, it will serve to cover the stray broken capillaries and little bumps that I am loath to admit are, in fact, hair follicles. Hair has fallen out of the top of my head, but its cousins have migrated lower, taking up residence on the lower part of my face. It's so unfair. But I know it's not personal. Facial hair is an equal opportunity offender. I have, on more than one occasion at a red light, looked across traffic lanes and seen women driving BMW SUVs and Honda Accords alike checking for chin hairs. I've taken to hiding tweezers in handbags, in my husband's car glove compartment, and in our earthquake emergency kit. My sister and I have also made a pact: if either of us should fall into a coma, we've pledged to pluck each other's stray chin hairs while awaiting implementation of our DNRs.

I approach the least intimidatingly attractive salesperson on the floor. She has a sweet, open, honest face, and she's either

Mexican or Eastern European. I can't place her accent, because it's hard to hear her voice over my inner monologue.

"I've got a list," I repeat to myself like a mantra. "Stick to the list, stick to the list."

But before I can stop myself, I've announced to her that I am turning fifty this year. The admission of my age is an invitation for her to tell me how great I look. This is terrible, because I know that she knows that the better she tells me I look, the more she'll be able to sell me. This is a directly proportional equation that has played out with increasing frequency in recent months. Somehow, the phrase "You look great," offered with a convincing amount of enthusiasm laced with a tone that suggests ". . . but it might not last," is the currency that gains entry into my bank account.

Marte, maybe her name, tells me she's forty-five. She confides that she has been using an amazing fruit exfoliant* that makes her skin glow and that she always gets compliments when she uses it.

"The one thing I don't need is a scrub," I say firmly. "But you look great."

Now we're the best of girlfriends, we compare diets, and although I regularly lie awake wondering whether the hormones I'm taking are speeding me toward an early demise or just slowly poisoning my inner organs, I'm speaking with authority when I say, "You really need to be taking both estrogen and progesterone, as well as massive doses of vitamin D and calcium."

---

*If you've ever wondered if the fact that the majority of computer programmers are male actually affects your life, consider this: "exfoliant" is not listed in the Mac dictionary.

I See You Made an Effort

I started hormone replacement therapy after noticing changes in my physiology. Over a six-month period, not once but twice a month, I couldn't leave my house. It was like my vagina had slaughtered something.

Then there were the hot flashes. Nothing can really prepare you for the suddenness and completeness of the blood-boiling sensation except maybe a bout of dengue fever or listening to hour one of Rush Limbaugh's daily radio show.

But neither of those things was the worst symptom of peri-menopause. I was regularly morphing from my usual bitchiness into a raving bitch. I wanted to kill everyone in my house, the people who live next door, in neighboring counties, and in countries whose names I can't pronounce. As I recall, the exact words that sent me to a pricey Beverly Hills doctor were spoken in response to my son when he mentioned he hadn't begun his homework yet: "Fine, don't do your homework, if you don't mind being a MORON."

It also felt like the inside of my vagina was being sandblasted during any form of sexual activity. "Dry vagina." Two words that should never be in the same sentence.

On my initial visit to a Beverly Hills hormone specialist, the doctor handed me a compendium of supplements she deemed essential for menopausal wellness.* Complete with diagrams, maps, and intersecting circles, it was so complicated, I thought it was a

---

*I am always suspicious of anything labeled "wellness," a term that has grown to encompass everything from regular exercise to meditating on abundance.

schematic drawing of the Large Hadron Collider. She also suggested a regimen of lasers, lightening and tightening, injectables and fillers. It was so overwhelming, I went home and curled into the fetal position on the chance that the effects of gravity on the aging process might be retarded if I ceased all movement.

When inertia was no longer possible (it was time for the afternoon carpool), I slathered on my bioidentical hormone creams and started downing supplements by the fistful.* After a few days, I did feel less homicidal and suicidal. However, this new routine dovetailed with yet another perimenopausal symptom, brain fog, to create a perfect storm. I couldn't always remember to follow the regimen, and once you start outsourcing your endocrine system, you've got a hormonal monkey on your back.

A month into the protocol, I set off on a book tour. I arrived in New York but my hormones stayed in California on my bathroom counter, where I'd left them. I sobbed for two days straight while staying in a hotel room *other people were paying for.* Months later, just as I was starting to feel good about mastering my routine, the *Wall Street Journal* and *New York Times* published front-page articles on the very same day about the relationship between cancer risks and hormone therapy but came to diametrically opposing conclusions.

But standing at the department store counter, I feel compelled to pass along my limited and flawed understanding of the subject to Marte because my do-gooder humanitarian streak, coupled

---

*Neither "injectables" nor "bioidenticals" is in the Mac dictionary either.

. . . . . .

with what might be considered an elitist condescension, assumes that she might not have access to the caliber of doctors I go to—or *have* gone to, as I've right-sized my budget and now score synthetic hormones at a health clinic located under a freeway overpass in the dusty San Fernando Valley. Marte, maybe, dutifully nods as I fill her in.

I pull out my list and read off the product number I've come to replace. The liquid concealer I've come for is so expensive it costs the exact same amount per ounce as beluga caviar. Clé de Peau's silky cream foundation, B20 "GLO," runs $120 an ounce. Clé de Peau roughly translates to mean "key to skin," but it might be more accurately labeled "key to your wallet." For that price, you'd think they could afford the "W." While she reaches to retrieve it, I notice a second number on the label—"3500." Could that be the dollar amount they predict users will spend over a lifetime? Probably. But there's no time to do the math because Bobbi Brown's Sunburst lip gloss really does have a warm glow. Her Tropic of Nectar blush is so peachy, and its name might even be a nod to Henry Miller, and Laura Mercier's Terra Cotta lip pencil perfectly complements my fading lip line and it might be the key to my looking, if not younger, then just the best version of myself.

And 6,906 miles away, the Greek economy is collapsing; and 5,457 miles away, 20,000 public sector workers are protesting for a living wage in London; and 16.3 miles across town, my son is ordering a three-dollar public school lunch whose ingredients most of the mothers in my zip code would never allow inside the bodies of their precious offspring but that my child will eat because I cannot afford a private middle school where sushi is being served in individual bento boxes.

I shouldn't be shopping like this because I'm on the declining side of my earning capacity. It's possible that in the remaining part of my life, I will earn less money than I have made up until this point altogether. I am earning less, I have less time in which to spend it and yet I need more money. Much more money.* Besides the kid expenses, not to mention the essentials, like shoes and shampoo, after a lifetime of perfect vision, I need glasses. Root canals, colonoscopies, and regular osteoporosis screenings are required as well. There's also the money I have spent on age-related sports injuries incurred while trying to get the amount of exercise recommended for a woman of fifty. And although I am an atheist, the only way I can afford the longer life span that the supplements I can't afford are supposed to afford me will be to find gainful employment in the afterlife.

And sure, given all of that, I should not be handing over my credit card, but I am not alone. No, I'm just further statistical confirmation of "The Lipstick Effect." The worse economic times get, the more women splurge on small luxury items. Which is why, as I reach for the card, I review the list of things I do not and will never have the money for, now that I am a slave to my face.

I have never owned a second home; I don't really own my first home, mortgaged as it is. Never flown in a private plane, never

---

*When I started writing this chapter, studies showed that middle-class Americans will spend $235,000 on average raising a child, and that excluded college tuition, but by the time I finished writing it, the cost had risen to $241,000.

. . . . . .

holidayed in Turks and Caicos (had to look up the spelling of Turks and Caicos), and the likelihood that I will travel there is so remote that I'm not even sure where they're located, though I am aware that they're a spectacularly tony destination where vacationers' effluence gets whisked swiftly away but flows untreated into the surrounding waters, causing degradation to endangered coral reefs.

I've never purchased a designer handbag, never hired an interior designer or eaten at a Wolfgang Puck restaurant when I was paying. I also have never lived through a genocide, walked across Africa, or licked newspapers for nutritional value like Frank McCourt, although I was once tempted to lick a positive review in the *New York Times*. I have first-world problems, I know this, but they are still *my* first-world problems. It's not that I want any one of these extravagances or that I think these things will make me happy, but there's something about knowing I will probably never have them that's not unlike how devastatingly sad I felt when I realized the window for having children had closed forever.

I also kept buying tampons long after the periods ended, eyeing them wistfully in the bathrooms of younger women, until I contrived an actual justification to purchase. I reasoned that I should stock our bathrooms with tampons in case one of my son's friends needs one. I'm sure I appeared deranged, strolling down the aisle, gleefully plucking the package off the shelf, triumphantly plunking it down at the checkout counter. "No, thanks, I don't need a bag," I chirped and sashayed out of the store clutching my totem of membership in the lady community. At home, I carefully opened the package, removing a few so the girls wouldn't feel self-conscious about taking one. If I spend any more money today, it will threaten my Tampax budget.*

So as I hand over my credit card and Marte repeats that she really wants to show me that scrub, I am holding the line at the outermost layer of my epidermis. It's like Vietnam. Must not cross the seventeenth parallel. "No, I'm fine, but do you have any samples of moisturizers?" I say, as the realization sinks in that I have spent over two hundred dollars in less than five minutes. I must not leave without receiving something free, and moisturizers are the Holy Grail of all facial products. The sheer quantity of them on the market is astounding. Promising everything from age defying renewal to tightening, toning, repairing, rejuvenating and stimulating, the descriptions alone can restore your faith in the value of a liberal arts degree. The dramatically depicted ingredients range from the oceanic (seaweed, algae and fish oil) to the botanical (lavender, jojoba and *maracuja*).

Many of the products on the market advertise under the moniker "cosmeceuticals,"† a term that conflates cosmetics with pharmaceuticals. Often this refers to "biologically active ingredients," and despite the fact that the FDA does not recognize any such category, it has a ring of authority, but means nothing in this context. A frog contains biologically active ingredients; so do lima beans. So go figure.

---

*I'd also have a lot more money today if I could just get back the dollars I wasted on groceries, magazines and assorted toiletries I bought while trying to disguise my tampon purchases when I was a teenager.
†"Cosmeceutical" isn't listed in the Mac dictionary, but in this case, I like to think that the brilliant minds at Apple just drew a line in the sand at this nonsense.

. . . . . .

The saddest unguent on the counter has to be the tub of goop whose label is simple and to the point: Hope in a Jar. I have never purchased that one. It seems like the last stop on the line before I start making animal sacrifices and sleeping in a hyperbaric chamber. But I am not immune to the seductive powers of the adjectives and adverbs that promise miracles, and I have spent so much money, I deserve samples, damn it.

But she doesn't want to just give me a sample. No, Marte is personally going to make a sample for me. As she scoops a minuscule amount of a vanilla pudding–like substance into the smallest plastic container in the known world, I shudder picturing the factory that produces these miniature pods. I say a silent prayer that they're not sorted by the tiny hands of child workers, and I promise myself I will reuse them when traveling. I try to make my features appear interested when she recites the antiaging qualities of this particular elixir, though I know perfectly well I have no intention of ever purchasing it. Depositing the teeny treasure into my purse, I move toward the door, but she is following me and subtly blocks my exit, positioning herself by another counter, manned by a slightly more mature version of herself. Marte tells me that her colleague Older Marte will show me that fruit exfoliant. Cornered. Matronly Marte takes my right hand and begins rubbing a fruit exfoliant on my skin. It's mango, or pomegranate, or watermelon, and she's massaging and massaging this cucumber, or papaya, or was it sweet potato? I have no idea, because the circular motion is starting to make me feel nauseous. She stops scrubbing and for some reason the skin on my hand looks brighter, shinier, whiter—how did she do that? "It's

. . . . . .

only fifty dollars," she tells me with an inflection that suggests that she is handing me fifty dollars.

"Oh, that's a bargain," I hear myself say in agreement. "Only fifty dollars."

It's made by a doctor, a doctor from New York, she tells me in the same voice my grandmother used to describe men who were good marriage material—*a doctor!* Marte says to Older Marte, "Tell her about the deal she can get." They're double-teaming me now.

"If you spend two hundred dollars, you get this bottle of oxygenated, harmonized water for free."

My grandmother Rebecca, from Minsk, would have liked the sound of that water. In the summers during the 1940s, our entire clan traveled by Greyhound bus from where they had settled in Mobile, Alabama, a few hours to the north, to take the waters at Healing Springs. For centuries, the Muscogee people visited this site, where the mineral water was said to cure everything from dyspepsia to eczema. You would not only bathe in the springs, you'd drink its curative properties as well. My grandmother had lived through pogroms and the Depression, so she expected a lot of value from everything she purchased.

"But will it keep my vagina from being so dry?" I blurt out. The Martes look at me blankly. "I was joking," I say. "JK, as the kids say—just kidding." But they just stare at me and I know I'll be going home with Dr. Colbert's Intensify Facial Discs, because they don't know me or my sense of humor, because I said "dry vagina" and because she spent so much time on my hand.

This time the financial exchange is rapid. Surgical, really. In that moment, I recall shopping when I was a kid, my mother holding her breath as each credit card she'd hand over would have to be tried before a sale could be completed. I would look around, hoping no friends from school were there to witness this ritual. At forty-nine, I have discovered that age gifts you with invisibility in all but monetary transactions. It's also given me compassion for my mother. I have it covered, barely. Cash extracted, I leave.

Arriving at home, I rush upstairs past my teenage son. "I'm working on a deadline," I yell down to him, which is sort of true when you think about it. I immediately strip off my clothing and step into the shower, pushing aside the upside-down bottles of shampoo and body wash. I carefully place this jar, labeled "daily nutrition for skin," next to the one marked "transdermal, bioenergized resurfacing solution," which I purchased only a few weeks earlier. I take out a facial disc and begin scrubbing my left hand, wondering how many of the millions of American women born the same year as me are doing something similar at that very moment.

After only a few circular motions, it's clear that I simply have dirty hands. I am an idiot. Brown was never ever going to be the new black. I scrub my face hard. Remove another disc. It's more scouring than scrubbing at this point, applying so much force that terra-cotta-colored capillaries bloom on the thinning skin around my nostrils. *Thank God I bought that concealer*, I think as I head down to heat up a frozen pizza for dinner.

Marte must be at home by now as well. Marte, whose real name I may never know, because I too have worked service jobs under

. . . . . .

a "slave name," is heating up the casserole she made yesterday from scratch. She's boiling corn and steaming greens for her kids. Marte, who is actually twenty-nine, in all probability, didn't need my lecture on hormones and vitamin D. She's probably read the latest research and smartly decided to skip them all, and I hope she's working on commission, because she deserves it.

"KA-CHING" OR "CHA-CHING"?

> **Dear God,**
>
> **Is it "ka-ching" or "cha-ching"?**
> **You're so omniscient, you decide.**

I am no longer allowed to sing in front of my son. I can't ask questions about school, no queries about girls, can't look too proud or enthusiastic at ball games, and all public displays of affection are, of course, verboten. Must sit separately when taking him to the movies with his friends, must never be nude within a hundred feet of him, even if doors are closed, can't allow a sigh to pass my lips (too old), an "oy" is forbidden (too Jewish), can't make a loud sound in an enclosed space even if a shelf falls on my head.

It's all come down to starchy foods. I've been dragging myself out of bed every morning to get breakfast ready just so I can watch him eat the Aunt Jemima–brand pancakes I've mixed from scratch. But now he hates my pancakes, I chew too loudly, the timbre of my voice is grating and he'd prefer to eat alone.

Our sole discussion of any length in the last few months took place over the course of an eight-hour car ride down the California coast, during which time we debated whether the proper pronunciation was "ka-ching" or "cha-ching" when mimicking a cash register sound. This went on for six and one-half hours. The remaining hour and a half he was sleeping, and although unconscious, he still managed to communicate his disdain through hostile body language.*

The downhill slide began last year. I was instructed not to make eye contact with him on his middle school campus. Doing my best to walk while staring at my feet was difficult enough, but I once made the unforgivable mistake of waving hello, a gesture that was deemed way too enthusiastic. It caused so much distress I could only surmise it was the teenage equivalent of waterboarding. After that, I was instructed not to leave my car; instead, I was to text him when I was in his immediate vicinity. There was an occasion, however, when I was forced to address him in front of a girl who may or may not have been his girlfriend, and I cavalierly mentioned his (adorable) freckles. A teenage boy's appearance is a very, very bad and inappropriate topic for his mother. There is zero tolerance in this arena for teenagers. You might inadvertently use the adjective "cute" when "handsome" is the desired effect, or vice versa. I suggest treading carefully.

---

*Urban Dictionary says both "ka-ching" and "cha-ching," my son's preferred pronunciation, are cash register sounds. For the record, "ka-ching" has over four million more Google hits than "cha-ching." Ka-ching, baby!

On top of that, entering the immediate space of a teenager subjects your own appearance to a scrutiny I doubt Anna Wintour could withstand. It's hard enough to please myself, but a teenager's prohibitions include: do not wear any outfit that could be construed as either trying too hard, not trying hard enough, or classified simply as "trying." I found out just how discerning the teenage eye can be when I enlisted my son in a project rebuilding elderly veterans' homes that had been destroyed by Hurricane Katrina in New Orleans. I was going to introduce him to social activism and impress him with my knowledge of local fare while connecting him to the part of the country where I spent my early years. We'd work alongside volunteers from across the country, share beignets and étouffée, and contemplate the mysteries of NOLA, including the gender of the attractive, scantily clad women who walk the streets of the French Quarter from midnight to dawn. My teenager refused to eat meals at my table or work on my crew and declined to be photographed with me, all because I had the temerity to be wearing khaki work pants. What horrible crime did khaki commit? Was khaki responsible for the collapse of the euro, the decline of science education in America, or Hot Pockets? Later, when I asked what the most memorable part of the trip had been, he replied it was befriending Skunk and Sam, the resident cats at Café Du Monde.

Tonight, however, my stock will go up, I am sure of it.

I've scored something that no teenager who plays the electric bass can resist, an invitation to a private concert of a well-known indie band. But we're late-as-usual-Mom-why-can't-you-

. . . . . .

remember-where-your-keys are, and we're rushing to get out of the house.

Where are my keys? Good question.

I started losing track of them five years ago and gave up because I'd rather use my remaining brain cells to scour my memory for movie titles, obscure sitcom actors and names of the spouses of old friends. I'll catch myself punching the air with a triumphant "Yes!" when my brain has successfully located this mostly useless information. When recalling the theme song from *Laverne & Shirley* is a cause for celebration, your keys are really the least of your problems, but I don't tell my son that. I just repeat what has become my catchphrase, "I'm doing the best I can," and continue rooting around the kitchen.

"And this concert better be great, Mom."

"Oh, it will be. I guarantee it," I reply as we exit the house aided by a spare set of keys.

I have promised him something extraordinary so I can spend two hours in his company. If all goes as planned, he will realize that I am a great mother, or at least that everything I do, have done, and will do in the future comes from having his best interests at heart. I hope I can deliver.

I blame this entire enterprise on biology.

My friends with older kids love to regale me with tales of how things will turn around.

"Your kid will eventually realize your worth and you'll find yourself having a ball with him," they assure me. But most of them had kids when they were younger than I was. I had to do

......

theater in Off-Off-Nowhere-Near-Broadway theaters in my twenties, instead of having children like nature intended, and now I'm paying the unexpected price of going through menopause while my son is going through puberty.

So many aspects of my grandmother Frances's life were thoroughly unsatisfactory. Higher education was a privilege reserved for the boys in the family. Her choice of spouse was largely dictated by the onset of the Depression. On top of that, in order to work, she had to claim to be unmarried, as no employers wanted to hire women who might be about to get preggers. At least at fifty, she was rewarded with the pleasure of inhaling the milky, sweet smell emanating from the heads of her grandchildren. It makes sense that just as your estrogen flow is waning, you get a boost of oxytocin, often referred to as the "love hormone," from caring for your grandchildren. My mother, at fifty-three, was a first-time grandma when my sister gave birth to the first of her sons.*

I don't have the luxury of waiting for my son to grow up and say, *Now I get it, Mom.* I had him at thirty-seven. If my kid follows my lead, I'm going to have little ambulatory time to enjoy his appreciation. Tonight, damn it, he will see I am just a little bit cool, even if he hates me for it.†

---

*Evolutionary biologists have even called this the "grandmother hypothesis," wherein females, no longer fertile, survived because of their usefulness in raising young children. Wouldn't you just know it, even middle-aged *Homo habilis* females were struggling to remain useful and visible in society.

†Suggesting to him that teenage pregnancy isn't the *worst* thing that could happen is probably one of the most egregious age-related parenting faux pas I've committed to date.

· · · · · ·

The idea that a concert could bring us together seems perfect. We regularly listen to music on our computers and the iPods scattered around our house. Or so I thought, until I saw his list of favorite bands on his Facebook page: The Antlers, Deerhoof and Deerhunter. I had never heard of any of them. What is it with all the venison-themed bands? Clearly the window was closing.

"What exactly is this we're going to, Mom? Do you even know?"

"I'm not sure," I lie.

Oh, I know, I do. I have planned this outing for two weeks now, but I must withhold details, because the more he knows, the easier it will be for him to reject the experience. My friend Heidi's fifteen-year-old daughter, Eloise, produces a local live music series, which has gained a national following on the Web. We'll be part of a small group who has been invited to a taping.

The idea that my mother and I would have shared musical tastes when I was a teenager would have been laughable. During my childhood there was one record player in our household. I told this to my son when he was ten years old. He asked if I had taken a flight to New York when I left home for college or if airplanes hadn't been invented yet.*

Though we were secular Jews, the few records my parents had invested in on their limited budget were Jewish-themed. We listened to *You Don't Have to Be Jewish, My Son, the Folk Singer,*

---

*If you are intent on furthering the canard that forty is the new thirty, you'll need to do better than the blank stare I gave my son when he inquired what kind of computer I brought to college with me.

and Theodore Bikel's *Greatest Broadway Hits*, over and over. If I lose my short-term memory, a definite possibility considering both a grandfather and an aunt had Alzheimer's disease, I might just be left with Allan Sherman routines and Bikel singing "Edelweiss" from *The Sound of Music*.

When my sister turned fifteen, the record player migrated into her bedroom, and it wasn't until she left home for college that I inherited her music collection and my parents bought me an 8-track deck to boot. But we never listened to Steely Dan, KC and the Sunshine Band, and Elton John together in the way that iPods and iTunes have made music so portable. When I was sixteen, I saw Jethro Tull play at the Hollywood, Florida, Sportatorium with a group of girlfriends. It was the first rock concert I attended, and maybe it was the strobe lighting and smoke effects, seeing the only rock band led by a flutist, or that someone puked on my tan suede Kork-Ease, but it was unforgettable. This will be my son's first concert. And he is going with . . . me . . . his mother. If there is any generational marker of difference, this surely must be it.

Our destination turns out to be a cramped loft in Hollywood. It's hot and the place is packed with teenagers sprawled on sectional couches in front of a small stage where the indie punk band Titus Andronicus is warming up. We find two empty folding chairs on a riser one level up from the couches, where other parental-looking people are seated, as the two Web VJ hosts take their place in front of the stage. My son inches his chair away from mine and stares straight ahead, careful not to look in my direction. He's younger than these teenagers, but I sense he wants to blend in with them, so it is not without trepidation that I whisper, "Take off your baseball cap." I want the girls to see his beautiful face, but he won't do it, and I know I can't push him. After half an hour, when he finally relents and takes off the cap, I gesture to him with a triumphant raise of an eyebrow, but he lets me know that his decision had nothing to do with my suggestion, mouthing a silent *What?*—the staple of the teenage male vocabulary.

As the hosts move into place, I can tell they are not fifteen years old, but hired guns that appear to be in their early twenties.

The male host, an actor dude, is dressed in such a casual way, you know a tremendous amount of effort went into his appearance. It's hard to say which aspect of his façade is more studied, his offhand delivery or his attempt to grow a beard. Each delicate hair on his chin appears strategically placed to cover as much surface as possible.

The female host has features almost horsey enough to render her unattractive, but her hair is shiny and flowing and she's got a flattering leg-to-torso ratio. She's also wearing a silky halter top, held up, as if defying gravity, by tiny sparkling strands of silver. I hate her instinctively. I'm positive she was a cheerleader in high school and that I scored better than her on my SATs, at least the English part. She reminds me of the blondes in bikinis who bite into burgers, juice dripping down their chins, in Carl's Jr. commercials. She's cultivated a ditzy delivery and even gets the name of the band wrong—"Titus Andonicus!"—but no one corrects her. Is it because her complexion is flawless and dewy? I know I

. . . . . .

shouldn't be so judgmental, but one of the few things I've been successful at maintaining into middle age is long-held resentments. Diets, meditation practice and regular flossing were all passing flirtations, but my distrust of perkiness? Intact as the day I first noticed the difference between my doleful Semitic features and cute-as-a-button symmetrical faces.

My pal Heidi, who's seated near me, leans over and says, "That was you, right?" referencing my career as a television host. But I was never that girl. Tan, fit, appealing in a nonthreatening way. I've always rebelled against convention. In the eighties, I had dreadlocks. My hair was my anarchistic comment on our materialistic society, or I couldn't afford conditioner—maybe both.

Cheerleader Host turns the discussion over to the teens on the couch.

The first to speak is Maize, a girl with vintage thrift-shop style. She fronts her own band and expertly drops names of her favorite groups. After her, scholarly Cassiopeia lets us know she's aware that the group's name has been lifted from a Shakespearean play and asks about the role of metaphor in song construction. There's tomboy Dale, with her gender-neutral name, buzz cut and leather wrist cuffs, and my friend's daughter, Eloise. Eloise is simply attired in jeans and T-shirt, glasses and long straight hair. She has an understated authority. She thanks the band for coming and asks questions about their musical influences. I can only intuit that Eloise has watched her fair share of television and determined that Cheer Host could potentially broaden the series' audience to include Web-surfing males who enjoy burger commercials.

. . . . . .

The band starts to play and I'm convinced Cheer Host doesn't even like music. She's bopping perfunctorily, but I am mesmerized by her confidence. I gasp, realizing she's so attractive she might even go home with one of the band members.

The band is bursting with youthful energy. The only female member, Amy, a guitarist and violinist, comes alive when the band starts playing. Warming up, she had appeared doughy, but now she's jumping up and down and her joy is palpable and contagious. She's also wearing a bright red romper. The romper is an infantilizing one-piece short jumpsuit, something like an adult onesie. Once reserved for toddlers, rompers were a questionable fashion trend in the seventies that has been newly embraced by vintage-wearing twenty-somethings in Brooklyn.* Does Amy wear that for every show? Or does she have rompers in different colors, I wonder, knowing that my romper years are long gone and I will never ever be seen in one, unless portraying the mentally ill.

The lead singer, Patrick, is emaciated, with a rangy beard and mischievous eyes. He radiates an intensity just menacing enough to suggest he could easily be cast in the TV movie *Charles Manson: The Early Years.*

Do they have medical insurance? Has their van had its tires regularly rotated? How often, if at all, do they shower on the road? Will they continue as professional musicians or will this be a story they tell their kids one day about when they were in a

---

*The brilliant Lena Dunham, who appears to disdain even remotely flattering clothing when she deigns to dress at all, is often photographed in rompers.

. . . . . .

band and toured the country before selling real estate or opening a Guitar Center franchise in some suburban sprawl? Have they eaten today? Patrick looks really hungry. I imagine inviting him home, spooning soup into his mouth and packing him nutritious snacks for the road.

In yet another unmistakable mark of aging, I notice how damn loud it is. But not a single other parent is making a stink about it. Is it possible that they have each come with the same intention as me? I resolve not to be a killjoy and concentrate instead on struggling to understand the lyrics—yet another challenge that marks me as an oldster.

I'm annoyed. Patrick said this album (he said "album"!) weaves together a tapestry of historical artifacts, including Civil War battle cries and Bruce Springsteen, with current events. Wow, Patrick not only has ambitious musical goals, but he just referred to someone I regularly listen to as an artifact. I'm both incensed and intrigued. But it's futile. Can't. Understand. A. Word. Eloise and the teens in the audience know all the lyrics and are singing along.

As I watch them, I'm so glad that the ability to appreciate new music is a sign of neuroplasticity, because I am genuinely liking the band's sound. I'm not going down without a fight! In fact, I like it so much, though the lyrics remain beyond reach, I want to dance, so I stand up and start to move forward toward the stage, when an arm reaches out and stops me. "Don't move down front," says one of the dads I'm seated with. "They don't want us to be on camera." Like lepers, we must be quarantined. For the first time

. . . . . .

in my life the sobering realization sinks in that should my person ever be violated, no one would suggest it was because I had worn something provocative. No, it would be characterized as a hate crime against women.*

Patrick addresses the crowd. He speaks of the horror of war, which he learned about firsthand by viewing YouTube videos posted by musicians singing about war experiences they've read about on blogs written by poets in Red Hook. He tells the crowd he hopes that one of them will be able to change the world. He's not addressing me or the other parents. Why would he? I'm just someone's mom, whom they might register only if I was standing over them and my hair were on fire. And then probably only to text "PLOSWHOF" (parent looking over shoulder with hair on fire) "LOL."

I was a C-minus science student, but I think this is what Einstein meant when he theorized the existence of parallel universes. Age has spun me into an alternate universe, one that exists in exactly the same space-time, but is unseen by those who are younger. My writing will not be read by them, unless endorsed by someone their age and then viewed as a kitschy relic of the past. I will not be noticed by them unless I am in the company of someone younger. I am invisible. I can only hope to remain visible to people close to my own age and older, while young people are visible to all, as if illuminated by klieg lights.

---

*I should have recognized this truth at least ten years ago. That I failed to see this is no doubt an age-related delusional fantasy propagated by repeated exposure to the "You're not getting older, you're getting better" Clairol commercials in the seventies.

Except for Betty White. Betty White is visible to younger people. If the successful campaign to have Betty White host *SNL* was any indication, people enjoy having an old person around. When I was growing up in the seventies, Ruth Gordon was the designated old broad in films. She also once hosted *SNL*. Before that, there was Molly Picon. But there is a limit to how many old people young people want to have around. The campaign to have Carol Burnett host *SNL* never gained traction. Just one. One old person is enough.

As a teenager, I enjoyed afternoon schnapps with my octogenarian singing teacher. In my twenties and thirties I always had a cherished friendship with a teacher, family friend or older colleague at whose home I might celebrate holidays or meet up with them for an elaborate lunch—their treat, of course.

You don't want too many oldsters, that would seem too *Harold and Maude*–ish, like you had a fetish for the elderly. I remind myself to make a date with my current old person, Rachel, a widowed neighbor in her nineties. Maybe someday I could be someone's old person. But as I succeed in making out Patrick singing the lyric "Tramps like us, baby, we were born to rally 'round the flag," I realize I *already* am someone's old person. I've assumed the college students I occasionally hire to work as my assistants think of me as their more experienced peer, but no, surely they've noticed the many years between us. I am their old person. Of course, if my kid becomes famous or extremely successful in whatever field he goes into, I might receive a career boost or at least get a lot of dinner invitations basking in

· · · · · ·

his reflected glow. I make a mental note to push him harder in school.*

Amy steps up to the microphone. She adjusts her romper and begins to speak.

"When I was fifteen I thought the most important things were to lose ten pounds and what people thought of me. It took me twelve years to figure out that it was to follow my dreams and not to care what anyone thinks and stand by my friends."

I want to cheer for Amy because I'm still working on my self-esteem, but when I look to see what the couch girls will think of Amy's empowered statement, I see them nodding their heads casually in agreement. I have the feeling I've got a front-row seat to some kind of Darwinian adaptation taking place. Oh, brave new world that hath such confident young women in't.

I've no doubt misjudged Cheer Host as well. She's probably a rocket scientist, or at least much smarter than I am. I once had a similar job, hosting a music video program for VH1. I refused to refer to the artists by their first names; instead, I insisted on calling them Ms. Houston, and Ms. Carey. "Annabelle," the producer gently prodded me, "the viewers want to feel like they know these artists personally."

"But they don't," I declared with the defiance that being in your twenties, attending only two years of college, and dropping

---

*Recent studies say that 65 percent of grade school kids today will go into professions that haven't been invented yet. I take pride in having succeeded in making the perilously unpredictable acting profession look unattractive enough that my son appears to be inoculated against becoming a thespian.

. . . . . .

out can give you, "and I want to remind them of that." I held that job exactly one day.

Cheer Host sees how to work the game, and that's a useful skill. I also never made one of those highly lucrative beer commercials, though I auditioned for them numerous times. No, I appeared in ads for Zima alcoholic beverages, whose flavoring resembled a cross between Kool-Aid and motor oil. During the time those spots ran on television, people would yell at me as I walked on the street, "Hey, Zima girl, that stuff tastes like shit, I want my money back!" I'm sure my son thought Cheer Host was hot, but even I knew better than to ask him.

The band starts to pack up their gear and the teenagers stand and casually begin to file out. I find it thrilling to be up close and personal with professional musicians, but this is the Internet generation, who take personal contact with the celebrated so much in stride that they have compressed the space between themselves and the band. This may explain why it is so hard to get them to fork over money for music; it's that old adage about familiarity breeding contempt playing out in its digital incarnation.

As we depart I ask, "Did you like it?!" but I have made the mistake of expressing too much excitement and am met with stony silence for the ride home.

In the car, I make one last attempt to bridge the gap between us. Cats. Not *Cats* the musical, but cats the domestic pets. Cats are his single enduring memory of New Orleans, and that's really the tip of the iceberg of how much we love the species. It's embarrassing to admit, but we were suckered into watching the cat being cradled by a gorilla on YouTube, the cat chasing a squirrel through

......

backyard tubing and the kitten having a nightmare.* Left to our own devices, we could watch all fifty-eight million cat videos consecutively. So I say, "You know, Meow, the thirty-nine-pound cat who was on a diet, died today."

My son replies in a witheringly dry deadpan I only dreamed of achieving as a comedian, "And how is that newsworthy?" I have to admit, I'm rather pleased that the critical-thinking curriculum at the overcrowded public school I send him to seems to be sinking in. I have to give it to him. He slinks inside, heads up to his room and slams the door.

Titus Andronicus, what was I thinking? I studied the play in college. It's the "punk" Shakespearean drama in which the queen of the Goths eats her sons in a pie. I've taken my only child to see a band named after this most tragic tale of motherhood. If he ever makes the connection, it could be the subject of a therapy session, if not another entry in the ledger I expect he's keeping dedicated to the many ways I am failing at parenting.

He maintains his first memory is of me accidentally closing his finger in his bedroom window, followed by my leaving his beloved blanky at an airport, but he really has no clue as to the scope of my missteps. For his thirteenth birthday, I surprised him by updating his bedroom. I purchased a sleek steel and wood storage cabinet and desk at a local vintage shop even though the dealer insisted on a hefty price, claiming these were "one-of-a-kind pieces." They were an instant hit. A few weeks later, I was checking out an office collective I'd been invited to join, and what

---

*Don't even get us started on the pattycake-playing French cats.

. . . . . .

did I see upon entering the large shared space? Two small end tables that were an exact match to my son's furniture. I tracked down the owner, Vanessa, who told me it was simply impossible that I had matching pieces because they were one-of-a-kind. It wasn't until I produced photographs of my son's room that she agreed to give me an explanation. It turns out that both she and the dealer acquired the furniture at a fire sale on the grounds of a mental institution in upstate New York. It was too much of a coincidence not to offer her cash on the spot. Carrying them up-stairs to his room, I notice the word "optimism" etched into the side of one of the tables. I have not yet nor do I ever intend to as-certain whether this sentiment was engraved by my office mate or by an inmate at the sanitarium, and I hope it wasn't carved using teeth or a toenail, but I'd rather not know. Furthermore, though I am well aware that inanimate objects cannot exercise willpower, it's tempting to consider that his bedroom furniture is deliber-ately conspiring to reassemble, at which point a malevolent chain of events will be set into motion. I must never reveal the unusual provenance or any of this speculation, as decorating his room is one of the few things he concedes I've done well.

I open my computer and find a song by the band. Their sound is addictive. I learn that Titus Andronicus the band has a higher listing on a Google search than *Titus Andronicus* the play, which is good news for me, because unless my son attends acting school, he will probably never know the irony of tonight's endeavor. I hear the same tune playing in my son's bedroom. I knock on his door.

"Hey, I just wanted to let you know that Amy went to Harvard."

. . . . . .

"Uh-huh."

"I found a YouTube of Patrick singing Lana Del Rey's 'Video Games' at his parents' house."

"I can't hear you, Mom, I'm busy."

He's listening to the band, texting friends and posting the pictures he took of Cheer Host's cleavage on Instagram.

In one last desperate move, I throw open the door to his room and do my best "Walk Like an Egyptian" dance move. There is something irresistibly pleasurable about embarrassing myself in front of him. "Mom, no!" he shrieks and puts his head down on his loony-bin desk to shield his eyes. At least I can still get a rise out of him.

I turn around, head back into my bedroom. As I pass through the hallway connecting our rooms, I catch a glimpse of nonagenarian Rachel gazing out of the picture window in the living room of her home just across the street. When she goes, there's only Mrs. Ho three doors down who's got a few years on me, then I'll be the Rachel. We moved onto this block when I was pregnant, and in a short amount of time I'll be the oldest person on our street. I'd better ask Rachel the secret to her longevity, because I am going to have to live to at least a hundred if I want to make regular eye contact with my son again.

THE SCENT OF PETTY THEFT

> *Dear God,*
>
> *If there really is an afterlife, can I spend mine in a plush bathrobe?*

The rich are different from you and me. Fitzgerald's line repeats in my head as I pull my dusty Prius into the driveway at the Beverly Wilshire Hotel. It has been years since I have been a guest in such an opulent setting, but I am neither intimidated nor overly impressed, because I am as comfortable at my corner burrito stand as I am in a five-star hotel. I have transcended class. I am an artist.

This is the narrative I have crafted for myself since I was nineteen and flat broke in New York City. I didn't see it then, but it was my youth, a certain amount of beauty—style, really—and the promise of a big career that allowed me to travel between classes. This combination can give you an all-access pass to the enclaves of the wealthy, but there is a time limit. There's a grace period you're allotted when the future is ahead of you, before people in your industry start saying things like *What happened to you? I thought you were going to have a big career,* or *I'm so impressed with all the ways you stay creative,* which translates to *It's astounding that your body hasn't been found decomposing in a fleabag motel in the high desert.* I am not becoming anything anymore. That's the kind of thudding honesty that occurs at fifty, and it's that kind of thing that can lead to petty theft.

I've arrived to discuss my duties at a charity event being held at the hotel that evening. I head into the bar to meet the producer of the event and it's easy to be friendly and breezy, primarily because I'm donating my services, so I can't be fired. There is a certain irony that I have been asked to forgo my standard fee at a black-tie event where most of the women will be wearing gowns that cost more than I typically earn in a month or maybe six. But it's a worthy cause, and I readily signed on.

We sit down in a cozy alcove on a silk damask settee and I sip what is probably the most expensive latte I have ever ordered. How do I know that? The price is written in Arabic. We're discussing the event but I'm distracted. Maybe it's because I'm shivering. It's as cold as a meat locker. Glancing around, I see that I am surrounded by expensively maintained skin, capped teeth and two sure signs of wealth: women with hair so blond and so immovable it can only be described as starched, and though we are nowhere near a body of water, 75 percent of the gentlemen present wear nautically themed jackets, brass buttons polished to perfection.

Monica, the catering manager, whom I'm introduced to, is professionally beautiful in the way that every woman working here today is. Tall, in good shape, but not so beautiful that she takes up space in your head. She doesn't even blink an eye when I blurt out, "Isn't this bar supposed to be a good place to meet high-end hookers? Which of those women are prostitutes, do you think?"*

"What? I've never heard that," she says.

It's an overshare, but I can't take it back, so I add, "Can I have your card? It's so nice to meet you." She hands me her card, and notes that if I need anything, to please let her know. "Oh, I will," I say, dropping her card into my bag, where it will join the bottom-of-purse lint—cookie crumbs, crushed vitamins, a crumpled notice from my son's PTA—until the day I change purses, maybe two years from now. I can't imagine why I'd ever need to call her except to ask for a job application.

I want this lunch to last forever. Bouquets of flowers are exploding from vases on both sides of our table. I am gripped by a sense of dread that this might be the last time I will be invited into a place where even the air smells expensive.

It turns out that it's not the flowers that are perfuming the air. Hotels have started pumping fragrances through their air

---

*This is the same venue where Julia Roberts hooked her way into Richard Gere's heart in *Pretty Woman.*

. . . . . .

vents to aromatically enforce their brand.* The Beverly Wilshire's aroma, Purple Water, has been designed by Asprey (the British line specializing in both jewelry and polo equipment) to reach into your reptilian brain and mimic the smell of old money. It has notes of leather, cigars and cooked peas. If an odor had corporeal form, Purple Water would be wearing an ascot. It taps a memory deeply buried in my subconscious.

Before my family moved to Florida, where I grew up, we lived in a series of small apartments in Wilmington, Delaware. The units had 1970s avocado-colored plasticky kitchens, and wall-to-wall carpeting, even in the bathrooms. That was an improvement from camping out at my aunt Gloria's house, where we landed after losing our home in Alabama. The Florida move marked a major step up for us. Our new residence was located on one of the exclusive man-made islands in Biscayne Bay, right off Miami Beach. A uniformed guard was stationed 24/7 at the gated entrance of the bridge leading to the islands.

I gleefully bounded into the house and lay down, pressing my face into the cool, polished hardness of the white tiles in the eight-hundred-square-foot living room. "We're rich," I reveled, though our cottage-style home was modest compared to the surrounding estates. Everything looked brighter here, from the tropical fruit growing in the yard to our future. It was like we'd

---

*The W Hotel chain, with its hipster appeal, uses a micro-mist diffusion system to infuse the atmosphere with a scent that's uniquely calculated to encourage the spending of lots of dough. W's scent, named Bling, calls up champagne, stainless steel and sex. Perhaps they harvested wrist sweat from Sean "P. Diddy" Combs during a VIP event and worked from there.

. . . . . .

been living in black-and-white and had woken up in Technicolor. I couldn't know it at age ten, but it was to a large extent an illusion. We were floating on a sea of debt. Our wealth was as artificial as the island we resided on.

We were also only the second Jewish family to move onto Sunset Islands. The first, a prominent local Jewish family, had to sue the Island Association to gain permission to live there. Upon our arrival, I made fast friends with Shelby, a longtime island resident my age. She and her mother, Gigi, were long, lanky blondes with sharp, birdlike patrician features who wore faded fruit-and-flower-printed A-line shifts. The whereabouts of Shelby's dad were never spoken of. Thirty-foot Doric columns framed their colonial-style mansion. There was little furniture, but even I could tell that it was "important." High-backed winged armchairs, heavy crystal chandeliers and leather-bound books. I thought it was fun that the only food in the pantry was crackers and hard cheese. That first summer, I enjoyed long sweaty days at Shelby's—they didn't "believe" in air-conditioning—polishing her mother's silver and skimming the leaves from their kidney-shaped backyard pool.

After my mother learned I was essentially working as a maid, the home was off-limits to me. I rarely saw Shelby again during the remainder of the eight years in which I lived there. They would drive by in their ancient wood-paneled station wagon, and I'd wave to them as they headed off to the Surf Club, a club whose membership excluded Jews, while I played touch football in the island park with the kids from the island's other Jewish family. Years later I recognized Shelby's colorful smocks as Lilly Pulitzers. Too bad I hadn't stuffed one of those dresses into my pocket while cleaning their silver. It might be worth something today. The smell of their home stuck with me, though. I couldn't put my finger on it then, but it turns out to have been cooked peas, cigars and leather—old money, in this case, really old money, so old it was barely there.

The hotel's Purple Water works its magic on me and I hear myself announcing that I'm going to be so tired after the event, I will need to stay overnight. Remarkably, the event planner agrees to this and after lunch I head up to my suite.

My hotel room is well appointed and maintained in a way that my home, built in 1932, will never be, with its corners that don't meet exactly.* Settling in the foundation leaves cracks in the ceiling paint and uneven gaps between the floor moldings and the hardwood floors.

There are no water marks on the suite's tables, no cats have sharpened their claws on the upholstery, and the walls bear no children's handprints or bicycle skid marks. In fact, the paint looks so fresh I have to touch it to determine it's not still damp.

A fruit plate has been placed next to my bed for my enjoyment. It's more like an ode to fruit. A perfectly shaped pear, two figs, and a grape rest on a single mint leaf inside a shallow Chinese porcelain tureen. It's so exquisite it seems wrong to eat such an elegent construction, but consuming it will be the only way to possess it, so I scarf the whole thing down quickly.

---

*Because very little in the way of updating has been done, my house provides visitors with ample opportunity to enthusiastically celebrate its "good bones."

. . . . . .

The room has not one but two balconies, and the bathroom is so sparkling clean I might be the first person to ever use it. It also has a feature I always think of as the true sign of luxury: a heavy door separating the toilet from the rest of the facilities. It's like Vegas: what happens there stays in there. In my own bathroom, mistakes were made. It was a full five years after I sprung for copper piping that water began leaking into the sink cabinetry. But why wouldn't it? Our contractor had apparently decided that replacing the old pipes would involve too much actual contracting, so he had wrapped the rusting aluminum in electrical tape. That was ten years ago. Correcting this remains on my to-do list. We simply have them rewrapped every year.

I open a bottle of Asprey hair conditioner in the bathroom and inhale deeply. I've got Fitzgerald's line stuck in my head: the rich are different from you and me and we will know them by their scent? I know that can't be it, but it also seems true. I proceed to stuff every single bath product into my purse and call down for more. It's a pattern for sure. I took home rolls of toilet paper from the nightclubs where I worked in the eighties, yellow legal pads from the offices of each TV series that employed me in the nineties, and there was that time I was sent to audition for the director John Hughes at a hotel in New York. I recall waiting in the foyer with an actress, whom I assessed as so plain, though I greatly admired her stage work, I was genuinely saddened that she'd never work in film or television. That actress was Cynthia Nixon. After John candidly admitted to not seeing me in the role, I thanked him and on my way out stopped to use his bathroom. I stole every amenity in plain sight and a few more from the housekeeper's cart in the hallway. I couldn't stop myself then and I can't stop myself now.

A card on the marble bathroom vanity reminds me that guests are invited to go to the spa, so I have to take them up on that as well. Who am I to turn down the invitation?

The spa changing area is paneled in dark mahogany, the lighting is indirect and muted and there are no windows. It's like a tomb, a bomb shelter or the inside of a bank vault.

There are cut orchids everywhere. There's even one in the pocket of the spa robe.

I enter the steam sauna, but it feels less like entering a room and more like I'm being drawn into it, like a black hole in space. I am the only person in the cave-like, serpent-shaped enclave. Tiny iridescent azure tiles cover the floor, walls and ceiling, the only light coming from pinpoint LED spots on the low ceiling that flicker from yellow to green and vary like the night sky. I've been transported to the Australian outback and am peering up at the stars. After a sweaty interval, I exit past a tiled wall where crushed ice is flowing into a polished chrome pocket on the wall. An attendant appears and inquires whether I am experienced. Is she making a Jimi Hendrix reference? No, she means have I tried the Experience Shower. It would just be impolite to refuse. My entire kitchen could fit inside this shower. I push the first of three buttons in front of me. This one is labeled *Atlantic Squall.* Streams of water lash my back; the pressure varies and moves from side to side like I'm being tossed in the middle of the ocean. I startle and turn when I feel someone's hand tapping me hard on the shoulder, but no one is there. It's the Experience Shower's many

. . . . . .

nozzles ratcheting up the pressure. I must be farther offshore now, as I'm drenched by torrents of hard rain. I begin to feel seasick. I saw *The Perfect Storm*. This might not end well! The lights in the shower area move from yellow to green to purple. Was the person who designed this on acid or in the employ of the CIA? It's like the Experience Shower is trying to get information from me. I switch to Caribbean Rain. It's a gentle sprinkle, falling softly, but it soon becomes chilly, so I select again and a slow swirl of warm Maui Mist envelopes me.

When I emerge fully Experienced, I check the full-length mirror to see if I've sustained any bruising, but I am intact. Pulling on my robe, I again think of that line—*The rich are different from you and me*—and then I remember the rest of the sentence—*and we will know them by their showers.* No, that can't be right. I know that, but my brain got jangled during the monsoon and it *seems* true. In less than five minutes, I've been drenched with enough water for several large families to cook and bathe for a week. How, I wonder, will I ever go back to my state-mandated low-flow showerhead with its 2.5-gallon-per-minute limit? But I can't stop to consider this now because there's a path of fresh flowers and candles leading to the Tranquility Lounge and I need to recover after my time at sea.

The lounge has chaises with fake-fur throws and dim lighting and new-age music that makes you feel something is happening, something essential, important, and you're not sure what, but it's a journey and you're on it. You're setting off on the Silk Road. The music is stirring and I feel charged with purpose, but there's nothing to accomplish except more pampering and there is a bountiful array of nourishing snacks, so I have to eat a straw-berry or two, or seven. I sip water infused with cucumber, also so soft. Soft, inside and out. Tomorrow, I will learn that at that very moment, in the harsh light of day, in a room buzzing with fluo-rescent lights, someone was yelling out questions and there was no guided meditation music, just charges of sexual misconduct being leveled against the serial sexting politician Anthony Weiner. But I am in a cocoon, and they just might have to arrest me to get me to leave. I close my eyes.

I know I can't stay in the spa all evening. I do have a job to do, after all, so I head to the locker room to dress, but somehow I take a wrong turn and head deeper in the spa. An attendant greets me, hands me another orchid and asks if I've made an appointment yet for a treatment. No, I haven't.

"Would you like an explanation of all the services we offer?"

I am curious, but always feel guilty in situations like this.* I don't want him to waste his time and attention on someone who can't afford to leave a gigantic tip or become a regular customer.

"You don't have to do that," I assure him. I want to whisper, "I'm one of you. I'm just working here tonight."

But instead of refusing, I let him walk me to view the five-foot purple amethyst crystal positioned in front of a purple glass wall that has purple water gently cascading into a small pond.

"The spa was built around this geode."

---

*I have friends who work as massage therapists. They tell me hotels are usually staffed by novices who've recently become licensed and receive low wages despite the whopping hotel fees. I feel like I should offer the attendant a foot rub or at least a cut orchid.

"Really? I thought it was built around a pile of money."

I later learn that amethyst is supposed to promote clarity of thinking. Maybe it works, because he lets my comment pass without even registering it. It's time to host the charity event, so I rub on every lotion I can find, then pocket a few disposable razors and travel toothbrushes, hoping they don't have hidden cameras inside the vault.

I head upstairs, change into my clothes and proceed down to the ballroom. It would be too tedious to explain my duties, but they involve two and a half hours of facilitating a panel about the preservation of wetlands that includes an elderly philanthropist, a noted film producer and an American alligator. One of them urinates on my lap during a spirited moment.

After the show, I see that mistress of efficiency, blandiful Monica, and ask her to point me in the direction of a bathroom. She says there is one I can use just down the hall. I follow a hallway that narrows until I'm practically brushing past the walls. The lighting starts to look different, dimmer, and even the paint looks less lustrous. The hallway ends in a stairway lit by a single naked lightbulb. Where am I going, Anne Frank's bathroom? I open the door at the top of the stairs. It's a restroom. It is not unlike other bathrooms I have used tens of thousands of times. There's a row of individual stalls separated by dented metal dividers and an industrial soap dispenser with a greasy pinkish film coating the pumping mechanism. Water drips into a rust-stained cracked sink, and rough, brown paper towels are stacked haphazardly in a pile on the grimy windowsill. It's simply outrageous. Where's my bathroom with the heavy door? Where are my

. . . . . .

products? It doesn't smell like any kind of money here, old or new. She's sent me to the bathroom for The Help. I am not The Help. I am a guest. I turn, march down the stairs, run out of that hallway and search until I find a hotel guest bathroom.

I didn't sleep at all that night. I would like to say I was kept awake horrified by my own self-involved, entitled, elitist behavior, but that would not be accurate. After dousing myself with more Asprey Purple Water, I lay awake because the pillow had my initials monogrammed into them. That's something I am still a little confused about. Do they keep stacks of initialed linens? Is there an algorithm that predicts the frequency of combinations, otherwise the linen closet would be immeasurably vast? Was my head resting on the same pillow used by Alan Greenspan? Do they remove the embroidery after you check out or was I expected to take the pillowcases home? It was truly vexing. Plus, I didn't want to waste one minute of how pleasurable the bedding felt by sleeping. The thread count of the sheets was so high they felt cold and creamy. The texture was not unlike what became one of my mother's signature dishes at our island home. Key lime pie, made with the limes from our backyard tree. The lime custard filling was terribly deceiving. It was so light, you'd be fooled into thinking you'd sampled a single bite only to find you'd devoured the entire thing.

It takes two, maybe three calls from the front desk to remind me of the checkout time. I take a shower and a bath. I suppose I subconsciously don't want to leave, because as I get into my car, I realize I've left my evening clothes upstairs in the room. The valet brings them down for me. I tip him ten dollars, even though that

. . . . . .

was six dollars more than I was planning on spending on a carne asada burrito sin frijoles for lunch.

The attendant asks me if there is anything else he can do for me. *Where do I begin?* I think. "Oh, nothing," I say. I head back across town, where the air is hotter, the streets are dirtier, where a sticky cough drop and half an Ativan can be found in my bathrobe pockets.

Arriving home to my block, I pull up in front of my neighbor's house. Our home was designed when families typically had only one car, and my husband has parked in our driveway, so today it's my turn to park on the street. These neighbors purchased right at the top of the market and have transformed their home into a spacious manse with a meticulously well-maintained native-plant zero-scaping, stone fountains, and imported olive trees that had to be lowered by cranes into the front yard terracing. I catch a glimpse of their sleek, powerful new Sub-Zero stainless steel refrigerator in their newly renovated kitchen. *Mon dieu*, it's got French doors.

On the other side of our home is Tobacco Road. The Joad family's home is sliding into disrepair; windows have been strangely and randomly blocked by metal stacking shelves, and bedsheets hang in the window frames, never a good sign. Our kittens jump over their fence and come home with oil stains on their foreheads. What's going on in that backyard, piled high with old furniture and car parts? They own a ten-year-old refrigerated truck, from the back of which they sell off-brand ice cream that I have strictly forbidden my son to eat. The truck is parked outside their house, where the patriarch of the family often works on it sans

. . . . . .

shirt and, neighborhood rumor has it, on occasion without pants as well. With the tangle of plants I like to call our English garden and our faded wooden shingles, I sense our house listing slowly toward Tobacco Road. When will our bedsheets go up?

I open our front door and it smells like teen spirit. I'm not sure what Kurt Cobain had in mind, but it's come to mean sweaty socks and FroYo, with just a hint of sunscreen, at my house. No one is going to take the aroma of our home and bottle it. I have bills to pay. I've got both horizontal *and* vertical cracks in the foundation of my house, but my bedroom is still bigger than any apartment I had in my twenties, potable water is only a few feet away, and I can still afford my own strawberries.

I will need to keep up that gratitude list practice. I vow to keep one of my dozen or so pilfered bottles of Asprey Purple Water body lotion on my nightstand as a reminder of how quickly I can be seduced. Also, because it smells soooo damn good.

828-3886

> *Dear God,*
>
> *Please don't ask me to kill again.*

828-3886. I recognize the number when I see it flash up on the screen. It's one of the few phone numbers that I know by heart. We've been friends for twenty-two years. Hers were the last digits I learned before we all outsourced our memories to our cell phones. All the other numbers from my past have lost relevancy or don't connect to the living: street addresses for homes we no longer own, birthdays of grandparents, channels of TV stations, prepregnancy shoe size, and of all those landlines long abandoned—hers was the last working phone number.

828-3886.

I answer the phone.

"Hey, Robin, what's up?"

When you've been close friends for over two decades, you can hear the bad news in the sound of their breath.

"Oh no," I say, bracing for the news.

"I have cancer."

"What kind?"

"Pancreatic."

"Pancreatic," I repeat in a voice I don't recognize. Or maybe it's a finality I haven't heard in my voice until now.

It had started as a slight pain in her abdomen earlier in the year. The initial diagnosis was gastritis. In recent years, Robin's greatest pleasures had been her wine-tasting group, gourmand weekends in Napa Valley and an annual trip to France. She'd even considered cashing out and hightailing it to a wine cave in the Loire Valley. After she triumphed over a lifetime of struggle with body issues, wine and anything worth eating would now be denied to her. It seemed impossible that "Cut out spicy foods and wine" had progressed to "Get your affairs in order" by springtime, but it had.

In my twenties, all cancers sounded the same to me, but I'm old enough to know that pancreatic is one of those no-one-gets-out-of-here-alive cancers. I voraciously consume the obits, tallying what takes out whom, at what speed and what the symptoms are, and I know that if Steve Jobs couldn't beat this one, nobody can.

Every time I pick up the phone, someone's having a health crisis. In the past, when friends have died it's seemed like the exception, not the rule, but now all bets are off. There was the cruel swiftness with which AIDS dispatched my gay friends in the eighties and then there was Fernando's overdose at thirty-nine; the actress who was murdered, leaving her young daughter motherless; the neighbor who'd dropped dead from a brain

. . . . . .

aneurysm on his daily run. Come to think of it, he'd just turned fifty. Now every passing year brings news of a friend's decline or demise. Last month brought a wave of suicides.

"Have you heard about Daniella's husband? He went off his meds and drove off a cliff. He left a note saying, 'I can't do this anymore.'"

"Two young children. Tragic."

"Did you know the comedy writer, Steven Something-Jewish?"

"Steven Something-Jewish, oh yeah, it was drugs and alcohol, right?"

"It wasn't career related, right, wasn't he always working?"

"Yes!"

"Tragic."

"Have you heard about . . ."

"Yes. Tragic!"

Deena's brain tumor, Yulissa's back surgery and Curtis's irregular heartbeat.

"Heart? Heart is good. Just look at Dick Cheney."

If I'm not filling out bring-them-a-meal requests, I'm dropping off medication, driving a friend to get an MRI, making an emergency sour cream run or walking someone's dog. People are starting to brag about their low cholesterol levels with the enthusiasm once reserved for sexual conquests. I hate that I get a joke with Boniva in the punchline.

But the news about Robin hit especially hard. She was the person I've known the longest since moving to Los Angeles. It can be challenging to make long-lasting friendships after college, but Robin and I had stuck it out. I leaned on Robin like an older sister

. . . . . .

in the early years of our acquaintance, when our five-year age difference seemed enormous, but over time, the gap had compressed and we'd become peers.

When my sulky movie-star boyfriend disappeared overnight and changed his phone number, it was her idea to drive out to a crummy strip mall and chuck the keys to his apartment into the sewer.* She knew me well enough to know that having those keys in my possession would be dangerously tempting for me, though in retrospect, I'm sure he had changed his locks as well.

Over the years there'd been times when I'd see that phone number and brace myself for the way her New Jersey nasal whine could inspire guilt in me. "Annnabeeeelle, it's Roooobin. Where are you??" But we'd put in the time. My divorce, her career setbacks, my career setbacks, my new marriage, her new career, the birth of my son, her big breakups, her parents' declining health. We'd been like sisters for two and a half decades and were heading into our third.

Our friendship was tested when she turned fifty. She'd woken up convinced that she'd been cheated out of the attention she deserved having never been married, with no children to birthday party or bar mitzvah. She insisted her closest girlfriends accompany her to sample Syrahs in the Rhône Valley. When none of us could take the trip, she felt betrayed and abandoned. Now, facing this diagnosis, she'd taken me and the rest of her inner circle back.

----

*I would never do this now, knowing that everything dumped in a sewer drains straight to the ocean, but it did feel great at the time.

· · · · · ·

"No one will ever have sex with me again."

"No one's having sex with you now. At least now you can attend your own group," I said in an attempt at humor.

After an award-winning career of producing stand-up comedy, Robin had gone back to school to become a therapist and had been working as a bereavement facilitator for oncology groups. She knew the landscape ahead of her: punishing rounds of chemo and if she was really, really lucky, she might get a year or two. Later it would make me apoplectic to hear people say, "It's ironic that a grief facilitator gets cancer."

"Not really," I'd counter. "That's like saying it's extraordinary when your doctor dies. What would be amazing is if they lived forever."

There was a certain excitement when she started the treatment, like the third season of a sitcom, when the characters face serious challenges but still fire off hilariously biting one-liners. It was just like Samantha's breast cancer story line in *Sex and the City*, except Robin didn't have a lavish wardrobe, designer shoe collection, sex, the city, or any chance of recovery. She did still have her sense of humor when she registered the domain name Tumor Humor. She was going to blog about coping with cancer through humor. Chemo was also a great excuse to purchase one or two new sweaters to attractively provide coverage for the port she'd need in her chest and cute fuzzy booties for good measure. Minus her gourmet cuisine and wine, her weight dipped precipitously, but we joked about how she was finally able to lose those pesky last *twenty*-five pounds.

After only a few months we went from sitcom to Lifetime Movie of the Week. Robin sprung for a human-hair wig styled after Elaine's *Seinfeld* season-six layered locks, so when her hair fell out, every day was a good hair day. Glowing from the chemo, she really had never looked better. But those good days didn't last. Her feet swelled up and the comfy booties had to be cast aside. The new sweaters hung loosely from her shrinking frame, her skin began to turn dull and gray and she still hadn't written more than a few paragraphs of Tumor Humor. Cancer? Not so funny after all. It was terrifying. For her. For all of her friends.

Is there something growing inside me right now that will eventually kill me as well? I've always harbored an irrational resistance to washing off fruit. I've purposefully, stubbornly re- fused to rinse it off. Why on earth do I do this? What's wrong with me?* Pesticides are undoubtedly eating away at my insides at this very minute, though statistically speaking, I will probably be bumped off by a teenage driver texting "What's up?" or the last thing I will glimpse will be tile. My friend the futurist and author Dave Freeman had worked his way through fifty of his Hundred Things to Do Before You Die that he'd recommended in his book; he'd survived running with the bulls in Spain and land diving in the South Pacific, but was taken out by a fall in the tub.

"The fifties are the weeding-out time," my friend Arye ex- plains. He serves on the pension advisory board of the actors'

---

*I always wash my son's fruit. It makes no sense, I know. I can't explain this self- destructive behavior.

union. "We could never afford to pay pension and health-care benefits if so many people didn't start dropping dead."

"Well, it's comforting to know they're serving a purpose for the greater good."

I'm a child of the 1970s: I saw *Logan's Run*, I know that Soylent Green is people and that if we lived forever we'd be unfairly stealing resources that belong to future generations. But when it comes to giving up your seat at the dinner table, most of us prefer to linger for one more coffee and dessert.

Robin wanted to hang on as long as possible, and she needed our help to make that possible. With no spouse, no children, she had only her friends, her chosen family. She didn't want to return to New Jersey to her mother with Alzheimer's, father with dementia and a strained relationship with her brother and sister-in-law. Isolation from her home and friends would kill her faster than the cancer and make any time she had left miserable, she reasoned, and the troops assembled. Neighbors began dog walking and handled the food shopping. Roommates from college, comedians and members of her wine group showed up to bolster her spirits. Her closest friends began coordinating and accompanying her to doctor's appointments and chemo, and even sleeping over on a regular basis.

I tried to carve out my usefulness. Her last relationship, with a foodie who had run a bacon-of-the-month mail-order business, had ended two years before. He left her with a Viking oven and a large collection of wines, but without hope of entering into another relationship. I decided I would start touching her as much as possible. We'd smoke her medical marijuana and then I'd wash

. . . . . .

her hair. She'd put her head in my lap, and I'd stroke her head and massage her feet.

Within eight months, we were in Bergman territory. Every time I'd leave her, we'd say good-bye not knowing if this would be *that* good-bye. There were so many farewells that she was starting to tire of them. It was gut wrenching.

"You're losing me, but I'm losing everyone I love all at once."

Robin couldn't tolerate even the most soothing of music, watch television or read, and barely rose from her bed. Hospice workers began twenty-four-hour shifts.

Every day I began bracing for the call that would tell me she had passed, but it didn't come. I was performing around the country and each time I'd see 828-3886 flash on my phone, I'd answer with the same question. Is this the call? "It's not *that* call, but I think you should come over when you get back in town and say good-bye," one of her caregivers would say. As soon as my plane would land, I'd drop my suitcases at home, drive to her place, hop into her bed, massage her bony shoulders and lead her through a relaxation exercise I learned from a rabbi. We're both atheists, but what harm could it do?

"Picture yourself lying on a beach. The sun warms your body. You know, Robin, we should really take you to the beach now that you don't need to worry about skin cancer! Imagine your soul rising up into the atmosphere, even though there is no soul separate from the body. Did you know that it was only after people realized that the body deteriorated after death, they needed to conceive of something that was separate from the corporeal body in order to support the idea of resurrection, and that's how the concept of the

soul being untethered to the body became an accepted belief?*
Anyway, 'you,' whatever that means, rise up to the clouds to Gan
Eden, the Garden of Eden, your soul's true home. I prefer concrete under my feet, but whatever works—maybe it's Bergerac or
Cahors. Everyone you love and who loves you is waiting for you. I
suppose that could be two separate and distinct groups of people.
I'm not sure what happens if your grandmother would prefer not
to spend the afterlife in the company of your grandfather, which
I'm sure is true in my family, but maybe the way it works is that
these 'souls' get together to greet you and then they go off to their
own corner of heaven with the people they'd prefer to spend eternity with—anyway, you greet your loved ones and you're surrounded by love. You're surrounded by love, Robin. Let go of any
stress you're feeling. Let go. Just let go. Now, slowly return back to
your body in a more relaxed state," I'd repeat.

I'd been doing this meditation in times of stress for years, but
it wasn't until I lay in Robin's bed that I realized it might actually
be a preparation for the Big Relaxation and that it might not be a
bad idea to skip the part about returning to your body, but I
couldn't bring myself to do that. She didn't need me to decide for
her when to go.

The words of the dying hold a special power. Famous last
words are oft quoted, even if they aren't true. *Jefferson lives,*

---

*I am paraphrasing Stephen Cave's book *Immortality*. I am very suspicious of this
idea that your ancestors greet you in the afterlife. I've always envied other people's
families, and surely I'm not the only one, but you never hear, "And when I passed
through the white light, there were the Millers, my old next-door neighbors, waiting
to greet me." How come?

. . . . . .

John Adams supposedly proclaimed, the rivalry between these two Founding Fathers following him to the death. I imagine his real last words were probably *I'm so uncomfortable . . . water, hot, where?* Some non sequitur. But we like this idea, the it-all-makes-sense-now moment that connects you to the dying, which gives their life meaning and in turn gives your life meaning and thus It All Makes Sense. I'm not going to lie and say these were her last words, but during one of these last visits, she clutched my hands and these were four of the last words I can remember her saying to me.

"Learn from my life."

I nodded my head, cried, and promised I would in the way that you do to the dying.

But what did she mean? *Learn from my life?* She should have married Bacon Man? Would things have been different? Would years of consuming even more pork products have sped up or slowed down what might have been the inevitable? Should she have moved to France? Would she have gotten pancreatic cancer if she'd taken up residence in a wine cave? Wouldn't we be having the same conversation in a room with fewer windows?

Learn from my life.

The only thing I was learning was just how much suffering a relatively small collection of fast-growing cells can cause.

Soon, she wasn't eating and didn't want visitors, just the inner circle. She was wrung out. We all were. It was bleaker than a Lars von Trier film. It was a Friday morning when 828-3886 appeared on my cell phone.

"Is this the call?"

. . . . . .

"This isn't *that* call, but Robin says she needs help and this is the weekend she wants to do it." It was another member of her inner circle. I didn't think twice. I told my husband and son I didn't know when I'd be back, packed an overnight bag and rushed out of the house. I knew what was being asked of us, even if it wasn't spelled out. We all did. This was going to be The Good Death, carefully orchestrated, carried out by loved ones. One by one, her five closest girlfriends arrived and the hospice worker retreated into Robin's spare bedroom.

Robin was skeletal. I would never have recognized her if she weren't propped up in her own bed. She was dressed in a white nightshirt. Her sheets and blankets, all white. We gathered in her bedroom. This was the group that never made it to France with her. The air was charged with adrenaline and sorrow. Later I would wonder if we weren't all anticipating the relief that soon this ordeal would be over for us as well. One of the girlfriends opened up a bottle of Drusian Prosecco.

"I hope that's not my good stuff," Robin hoarsely whispered.

"What are you saving it for!?" we all said at the same time.

We toasted her. We kissed her. We told her we loved her. It really felt like a celebration as we started upping her pain medication.

The plan was vaguely expressed to me, but as I understood it, she would fall into a coma and her do-not-resuscitate order was in place. I wasn't really clear on the legal ramifications of what we were doing—I'm still not—but each of the five of us pushed the pump as we stood by the bed. Each one of us wanted to make sure our fingerprints would be on the button on the morphine drip. We didn't want any one person to be culpable.

"We should really confuse things—let's put the dog's paw on the pump!" someone exclaimed. It might have been me—I think it *was* me, but it was hard to tell; we were giggling and crying and working together as one unit.

This is exactly the way I want to go, I said to myself: in a circle of love.

By this point she had Paxil, Wellbutrin, morphine, oxycodone and Haldol in her system and still she was totally lucid.

"You're incredibly drug resistant," someone said. "You should have done heroin!" Okay, I said that. Her first job out of college had been as a page on *Saturday Night Live,* working with some of the great drug addicts of all time. Oh, the parties she'd excused herself from. If only she'd known. Was this the learn-from-my-life moment?

We sat by the bed while Robin dozed on and off for the next few hours, but she wasn't going under. Every time she stirred, all five of us would jump to help. If she wanted her mouth swabbed or needed to throw up, we attended to her needs. If someone had told me the night we met in 1989, throwing back drinks in a Century City screening room to celebrate the comedy special that she'd produced, that one day I'd be pumping morphine into an IV drip into this vibrant woman's arm, I would never have believed it.

"I finally have my big Hollywood moment. If I get an itch, I have five people to scratch it."

. . . . . .

It was almost midnight when we began to make plans for the inevitable and we realized we faced a twenty-first-century predicament. We didn't have the password to her computer. I suggested "Languedoc," a wine region in France that Robin loved and that's hard to spell but awfully fun to say, but that didn't work. We tried the name of her niece, other grape varieties and even artisanal cheeses—Mothais, Idiazabal and Zamorano. Nothing.*

"Wake up, Robin. You can't die yet, we don't know your password." I shook her awake. She looked at us and with perfect deadpan comic timing, she told us, "It's Robin."†

We puffed her pillows, smoothed her comforter and settled in for the night. I stretched out in the hallway outside her bedroom with another friend. The other three women were camped out in the living room. A baby monitor was turned up so we could keep tabs on her. It was three a.m. when we heard her. She was close to falling into that deeper level of sleep that would lead to the big sleep, but she kept rousing herself. She called. Two of us went in to her.

"I need to get up and walk. I need interaction," she said as she tried to lift herself up.

"No, Robin, you can't get up," my cohort said flatly.

---

*Though I made up my mind that if I ever decided to adopt triplets I couldn't do better than those names.

†It's a good idea to write down the password before someone comes to your house to help you exit this world. If you don't do it when you read the meditating chapter, do it right now—stop reading and do it, then email it to at least two friends. If you're worried about hacking, write the passwords in a separate email from the account numbers. Have I done this? No, but don't be like me—learn from my life!

. . . . . .

Something inside me went numb. I said nothing. Silently, robotically, I shifted her position on the bed. I tucked her in tightly. I turned my back to her. I walked out of her bedroom and closed the door behind me.

Only later would I remember how utterly fragile she looked. How totally dependent she was on us. How her bony hands had pulled at her nightshirt to cover herself when I moved her. How her swollen genitals were a shade of deep purple, like raw liver. How her attempt at modesty was the last gesture I would witness from my friend of twenty-two years.

No more for you. That's what we were telling her and telling ourselves. I hadn't gently guided her to "just let go." I'd cut her off. What is the right word for the complete absence of anything funny?

It did not All Make Sense, and she couldn't let go. Just let go. By seven a.m., after a fitful sleep, one of the girlfriends realized we had a problem. Or, rather, we were the problem. "She's not going to be able to do this unless we leave; she's going to keep reaching out for us and it's only going to get harder. On all of us," she said. One by one, we departed.

The call came the next morning. Only the hospice nurse was at her home at the time of her death.

During the days that followed I became furious with Robin. Why did she ask this of us—I wasn't even her "real" family! I'm a comedienne; I'm the last person you'd want to decide when and how you should depart this lifetime. Maybe I'd misunderstood what she'd wanted, she was on so many drugs. Maybe what she'd really wanted was for me to beg her to hold on and keep fighting? Why hadn't I said good-bye when it really was the time for good-bye? It was supposed to end in a circle of love! I was racked with guilt.

Robin's obituary read that she'd fought hard but lost her battle with cancer. *Learn from my life?* One thing I learned is that if I ever get cancer, I'd prefer it chronicled like this: she lived it up as long as she could, then bitched and moaned and cried and cursed her fate like everyone who has cancer.

Her blood relations arrived to close up her affairs, pack up the family silver, the china and the good jewelry. They oversaw the selling of her town house, but her voluntary kin were left with the job of cleaning out her sock and desk drawers, dispensing with the detritus that the dead leave behind.

It felt dirty, pawing through her closets, looking for something to take to remember her by, especially after hastening her death. But what? Her shoes had scuffs on the bottom, the inside linings of her purses were stained and torn. I'd always thought of her as well dressed, but everything in her closet looked tired. The majority of your possessions will immediately lose any value when you die, especially clothing and shoes. Maybe that's what she meant by *Learn from my life. Would anyone want this after my death?* is a question I ask myself every time I go shopping now, and it regularly saves me from buying stuff I don't need. I took home the books that I'd authored and had inscribed to her, along with her collection of inscribed books from other writers. I couldn't bear to think of them ending up in an anonymous thrift store, though it's likely her books, along with the contents of my bookshelves, will end up there one day in the hopefully distant

. . . . . .

future. If the future is completely paperless, my books, which now include Robin's copy of *Live from NewYork: An Uncensored History of Saturday Night Live* in which her name is spelled incorrectly, will spend eternity decomposing in the Puente Hills landfill just outside of Los Angeles County. I left with a few choice bottles of wine in tow.

Witnessing the passing of our friends, our pets, and our heroes is increasing in regularity and is giving rise to all manner of negotiations. Especially regarding our own demise.

I met up with my single friend Lauren for lunch and when I inquired how she was doing, she blurted out, "I don't want my cats to eat me. I really need to get married."

"If there's ever a stretch of time when I haven't heard from you for more than two days, I'll stop in and make sure you're still alive," I promised her.

"When we can't wipe our asses, or if we forget who we are, let's make a pact, we'll jump off a cruise ship together," Gia, my attorney, who is the same age as me and a fan of Jonathan Franzen's *The Corrections*, suggested in an email.

"We'll have to make certain we're really far out to sea. If we're too close to port, we might hit the bottom and break a leg."

"Yes, that would be even worse, a broken leg on top of everything else."

"Right. And, Gia, if I kick the bucket before you, take my suede Stuart Weitzman boots. I just had them reheeled."

After a few weeks of watching me suffer, my husband, Jeff, said, "You did the right thing, but I don't think I want to be left alone with you if I'm ever really sick."

. . . . . .

"Thanks a lot."

"Come on, let's toast to Robin. She'd love that," he said. We opened a Benton-Lane 2008 from Robin's collection. Jeff was the first to take a sip.

"It's undrinkable—it's turned."

We opened a Château de Claribès Sauvignon Blanc 2009. Same thing.

The Russian River Pinot Noir had cork rot, so we couldn't drink that one, either. Thank God she never knew. It would have killed her.

MARAUDING THROUGH THE MIDDLE AGES

> *Dear God,*
>
> *Please keep my head from catching on fire.*

Comparing where you were in your career at thirty to where you are in your career at fifty is not advisable in any profession, but it's especially a bad idea when it's midnight and you're emailing pictures to a Hollywood casting director to prove that you can easily pass for a middle-aged woman from the Middle Ages. In the middle of the night. A trifecta of middle. "I was born to crone," I write in the subject line, adding three exclamation points to demonstrate my unbridled enthusiasm. I wash every trace of makeup off my face, turn on a bright overhead light and start taking pictures.

Earlier in the week I attended a DirecTV commercial casting

call to play a "real to slightly character-looking, approachable, believable mother." *I've got this one in the bag*, I reasoned. "Real to slightly character" should mean "could be Jewish." I have given birth, and if my hormone cocktail is calibrated just right I am capable of appearing approachable enough that I won't bite anyone's head off for limited increments of time, especially if someone is paying me. Plus, I know there are probably only several thousand women in Los Angeles that fit this bill and out of those several thousand there are only several hundred who haven't married into fuck-you money, or gotten their real estate license and dropped out of show business. Figuring in the ones who aren't picking up or dropping off their kids, felled by the flu or recovering from plastic surgery, I anticipate there will probably be only a hundred women who will be able to go in on the call.

I'm pleased to have been called in to play a mother, as this is a category that I am quickly aging out of. At this age, many auditions are for pharmaceuticals. This can lead to strange exchanges with your agents, who need to ascertain if you, in fact, have the disease being treated, which is sometimes a legal requirement.*

"Damn it. I don't have mesothelioma. Is the commercial for cable and Internet use, too?"

"And print ads."

"Is it something I could contract before Thursday?"

My actress friends and I were both thrilled and horrified to find ourselves auditioning for a product that treats menopausal

---

*I've been pining for a Cialis spot so I can get the Eli Lilly bigwigs to explain that enduring two-bathtubs mystery.

dry vagina. "Let's ask them to pay us in a lifetime supply," we laughed, and then some tears were shed. "Are we there yet?" Yes, we are.

I decide to make an effort. "Making an effort" is one of the punishments of age. In my twenties I went to auditions in my pajamas. My blasé appearance was a rebellious declaration of non-conformity. If I did that at fifty, people would assume I'd suffered a break with reality and I'd be escorted off the premises by security guards.*

I carefully choose a cheerful red polka-dotted dress; the polka dots I hope will communicate "character," perhaps reminiscent of Lucille Ball, and the red should add the right amount of color to my face so I can look youthful enough to fit into the "mother" category. At commercial auditions, you are expected to come dressed for the part. If the spot called for Satan, any number of casting directors would click their tongues and shake their heads in disgust if you didn't show up with horns protruding from your forehead, a forked tongue, and a tail. If the role is for a medical professional, actors will show up in scrubs with stethoscopes casually draped around their necks, so it is unsurprising that the other women at the audition and I all appear vaguely related and similarly attired.

"I see you made an effort" is how my hairdresser greets me

---

*Larry Charles, a *Seinfeld* writer, is famous not only for his brilliant writing but for wearing pajamas to work. It was rumored that Mary-Louise Parker used to roam the streets of New York in the eighties in a leather jacket that had FUCK ME, I'M A STARLET written on the back—I hope that's true; she's always been a take-no-prisoners artist destined for stardom.

when I stop for a fresh blow-dry, even though it stretches credulity that an actual mother would be freshly blow-dried, but this is TV, and all TV is aspirational. Unless it's reality TV, and then you must appear as derelict as humanly possible or decked out like a Kardashian Barbie because reality TV is produced solely as an excuse for viewers to enjoy feeling superior to rednecks, pageant contestants, hoarders and housewives with hair extensions.

The majority of these individuals fall into a category I think of as "celebrilites." These media-created personalities have typically accomplished little worthy of celebration, other than keeping themselves perpetually in the public eye, if that can be considered an achievement. They occupy a claustrophobic subset of society, socializing with solely each other, cross-promoting each other's clothing lines and cookbooks. In the same way that high levels of lead in pottery have been linked to the decline of the Roman Empire, I would venture to say that our exhaustive fascination with celebrilites heralds the decline of Western civilization more than even the popularity of Funyuns.* A small accomplishment I celebrate is that in my forty-nine years I have yet to invite cameras to document me splashing white wine on the masklike face of a celebrilite in a cookie-cutter McMansion.

Two days later I hear I have gotten a callback for the DirecTV spot. This one is mine, I'm confident. All I have to do is stand in a kitchen and rub my nose. I've stood in kitchens. I've rubbed my nose. Many times. I expect to rub it again in the future, so why not

---

*It's worth noting that the snack food Funyuns has as much in common with an onion as a bar of soap. The main ingredient is cornmeal.

with a camera rolling? At the callback, a group of thirty actresses in my category are corralled into a holding area. At least three of us are wearing identical red polka-dotted dresses. We are informed that the director and ad agency executives will be in the room. We are to speak our names into the camera. The director will then point to us and either say yes or no, and if it's no, we are instructed to leave the room. If yes, we will be granted the privilege of rubbing our noses.

There are more actors than chairs, it's stiflingly hot and we wait for over an hour before they start the weeding-out process. Some are pacing anxiously, nervously reapplying makeup or rehearsing. I seize the opportunity to catch up with acting buddies. I have just enough time to find out what sports my friends' kids are playing to keep my spirits from flagging. Too much introspection at such moments can be a dangerous thing.

Projecting into the future must be avoided at all costs. I've caught myself adding the words "for the rest of my life" to the end of sentences—a twist on the Chinese fortune cookie game, the one where you add "in bed" to every fortune you get? You will enjoy unparalleled success . . . "in bed." You will make new friends . . . "in bed." That pillow-crease wrinkle on my face that used to disappear an hour after waking will remain there . . . "for the rest of my life." One bad landing on the tennis court and I could wind up in the boot . . . "for the rest of my life." A job interview where I can be disqualified after merely uttering my name is the best I can expect . . . "for the rest of my life." Even if it's true, I've had to institute a zero-tolerance enforcement policy.

Reviewing the past is a luxury I cannot afford. It's a stupid

. . . . . .

trap that can catapult you into a depression that will send you packing to an ashram in the Catskills or opening an Etsy store selling sculptures made from chewing gum. I am auditioning for a role in a commercial, I tell myself. It's not glamorous; it's like being a plumber. You are filling a need, and sometimes you're working with crap, you're just not as well paid.

This is how I made a living at the onset of my career. I was excited when picked to be in the company of "Grapes," "Apple," and "Leaf" for a Fruit of the Loom commercial in the 1980s. After all, Academy Award–winner F. Murray Abraham had famously played "Leaf" in a series of the spots. I sang about McDonald's "two all-beef patties, special sauce, lettuce, cheese, pickles, onions on a sesame-seed bun" with gusto, but I also made spots for local beauty schools and sketchy technical colleges. When you're on TV every week, you can negotiate generous endorsement rates, but I've come full circle and am back to auditioning for work at the basic union wages.

Many actors whose careers have middled like mine give up competing for these gigs. It's a numbers game and it can be soul-crushing. You might hustle to hundreds of auditions where you will wait for hours at a time, only to be instructed to act like you have a headache "this big," which you actually have now that you've waited so long to be seen, and still not get a job offer. On top of that, when you amortize the time it takes to get a single job by the daily rate, it doesn't make financial sense unless the commercial runs often, which is when the real money comes in, and you have no way of knowing if you have been lucky enough that

. . . . . .

the one you have booked will yield big returns. Years of training can seem completely tangential to waltzing around a kitchen to "Makin' Whoopee" while cradling a ketchup bottle, but I was certain that my Heinz salsa-style ketchup commercial was going to rake in big bucks. This was in 1993, when anticipation for salsa-style ketchup was being touted in the press and it was positively infectious. There was so much excitement on the set you would think we were making the sequel to *Citizen Kane*. As it turns out, people like salsa and people like ketchup, but people like to enjoy them separately, and the commercial was quickly pulled.

Still, I have always enjoyed the actual work, even though commercial acting, in the pecking order of show business, is the near lowest rung but for background work. Background performers, "extras," are viewed as scenery that requires bathroom breaks at inconvenient moments.* The hierarchy could be calculated something like this:

Tom Cruise *is* some very intense heroic character

Movie star

TV star

Reality TV star

Series regular

Cameo

Guest star

---

*Except by Harry Shearer, who has hilariously given out Best Background Actor awards on his radio program, *Le Show*.

. . . . . .

Costar

Sober companion to a recently rehabbed star

Former reality-TV star

Recently deceased television star

Starbucks barista

Commercial actor

Sloth

Background performer

Actress over the age of fifty

With my hair blown dry again and bright costuming, surely I have at least as good a chance at getting this gig as a recently deceased TV star.

Five actresses walk into the room with me. I am the first one to say my name. Smiles frozen on our faces, we hold our breath as the director makes his pronouncement: "No, no, no, no, yes." I file out of the room on wobbly legs along with three other actresses. We are dismissed. As we gather our coats and purses, we attempt to laugh it off, shrug our shoulders and return to our lives, but I can't believe it. I made an effort. That's when someone emerges from the room. He strides toward me, past a group of defeated-looking, slightly paunchy men who are all wearing bathrobes. They must be here for a husband role.

"Annabelle, it's Dan, Adina's friend, from New York." With his cashmere sweater, expensive watch, loafers and pressed jeans, he's definitely dressed too upscale to be auditioning.

"Oh, Dan, hi." Dan and I have met several times over the years through Adina, a mutual friend in New York. I hadn't recognized

......

him among the sea of faces who hadn't introduced themselves or even greeted us in the audition room.

"This is my account. I'm so sorry, that's just how the director is."

"Oh, no problem," I say, trying to appear unaffected. The last time I saw him we were seated together at a dinner party; now I was just another actor vying for employment. "How long are you in town?"

"I'm not sure, we've got one more session. We're casting for villagers."

"You mean like, 'It takes a village' villagers . . . a group of mothers?"

"No, our story takes our modern dad into the Middle Ages, where we need marauding villagers."

"I can maraud," I announce.

"But we need people who look unkempt, disheveled. Unless you were royalty, the Middle Ages were really tough on people," he says.

I would like to point out how hard the middle ages are on 99 percent of us in this day and age, but I'm trying to get a job. "I made an effort," I blurt out. "Marauding villager, that's my normal."

"Okay, well, I'll see what I can do."

He emails later with the information that they haven't cast all the villagers yet, and that is how I come to be spending the evening sending pictures taken with my computer camera looking exactly how I did before I attempted to approximate a nice mom with an itch to scratch on her nasolabial folds.

. . . . . .

I See You Made an Effort

I wake up to the news that I've been chosen to maraud. I show up at the wardrobe fitting and am laced into a beautiful velvet bodice that the wardrobe mistress immediately covers with a bulky peasant blouse and shapeless skirt. She drapes a rough woolen tunic over the blouse and wraps me in a knitted shawl. I have never felt so ancient in my long life. My grandmother would weep. When I landed my first long-running role on television in the mid-1980s on the soap opera *Guiding Light*, playing a girl gang member, I wore a studded leather motorcycle jacket paired with a leotard and ripped leggings. She lamented, "I can't believe my grandbaby looks like a prostitute. Couldn't they put you in a nice twinset?" This would have killed her. I look exactly like my potato-farming ancestors from the Ukraine.

We are to shoot in the evening on the European street on the back lot of Universal Studios. It's exciting to pull up to the historic medieval town streets lined with small turreted brick buildings crisscrossed with wooden beams, stained-glass windows, and low tiled roofs, even if they are actually only stucco façades. I intend to maraud like there's no tomorrow. The entire area is swarming with crew members, cranes and a large cast of extras. A spindly biped with a felt dunce cap precariously balanced on his skull ambles by and tips his hat in my direction. His skeletal frame and impossibly long limbs give him the appearance of a medieval arthropod. I spot a wrinkled and stooped creature who appears to have gone through extensive special effects, with his sallow, sunken cheeks and half-dozen tendrils of greasy hair emerging from his otherwise bald head. I am about to

. . . . . .

compliment him when he smiles at me and I see that he has no teeth and is, in fact, heading *into* the makeup trailer. A group of rotund men with ruddy faces and long wispy beards wearing-lederhosen (their own?) are standing in a circle chugging coffee from mugs while leaning on pitchforks. It isn't their first time at this rodeo; some have brought their own stadium chairs. A gaggle of pink cheeked plump matrons who look like dumplings in ker-chiefs are lolling about the craft services table. The temperature is falling fast, the sun hasn't even set yet and there isn't an indoor waiting area for the background actors, just an open tent with a portable heater and metal folding chairs.

I spot one of the mothers from my son's school among the background matrons. She and I have worked on PTA events to gether, and from her obvious mortification at being recognized, I know that she must have her own long and winding road that's brought her to this evening. I invite her to come and hang out in my trailer, but that's before I learn that my own accommoda-tions aren't much of an improvement over the background hold-ing area.

When you're the star, you get a big trailer to yourself. It is often tricked out with several seating areas, an eat-in kitchen, and a bathroom with a shower. I've enjoyed those trappings. It can make it very easy to show up on set and do your best work when you've been comfortably preparing in your plush digs. For a big honking star, the sky's the limit. I accidentally wandered into Eddie Murphy's encampment when I worked with him on *Daddy Day Care*. There were several trailers, an outdoor lounge complete with artificial grass, private gym and basketball hoop. If you're playing a supporting role, you might be housed in a "double banger": this is essentially half the size of a star's trailer, but comfortable nonetheless. For commercials or smaller roles, you can find yourself ensconced in a trailer that's been divided into a row of narrow airless cubicles called a "honey wagon." These rooms are typically as luxurious as a prison cell. This particular trailer appears to have last been updated in the late 1980s; the only amenity is a transistor radio with a cassette player. It's actually little more than a bathroom stall. A padded cushion covers the toilet located at the far end of the five-by-ten-foot compartment. The sickly sweet smell of air freshener hangs in the air.

There are eight of us principals, and the producers have assigned two of us to each of these pens, which are a tight fit for even one person. None of us has ever been asked to share such a small space as all of us are experienced and accomplished professionals. Basically, it's like you'd held a position that came with a title and a corner office and are now back in the mailroom. On a trial basis.

As I stash my belongings inside our cramped cubbyhole, I'm thinking about how common it is now for people in their fifties and sixties to spend months fruitlessly searching for work, facing rejection and reinventing themselves with Plans C and D. Only that morning I'd read about an American woman who aged out of her career in business management. After several years of seeking employment, she'd been able to secure a position with a company located in Pakistan. She had to dress modestly, couldn't walk the streets alone, lived in a rooming house—and this was a *success* story! With my credentials, I couldn't even get a job in Peshawar. I've got to make this work.

Both the background and principals are hustled through hair and makeup together and I'm convinced the scowling makeup person is mistaking me for a background performer. She rubs dirt on my face and flattens my hair to my head with the heel of her hand. "You." She points to me as I exit the trailer.

"Me?"

"Yes, you. Go wash your face. You've got some mascara on, it looks too modern. You should never show up for work with makeup on."

"Okay." I nod sheepishly, mentally noting that the actress who has gone in before me is wearing iridescent blue eye shadow.

"I've got my eye on you."

We wait for the sky to darken so our nighttime shoot can begin. We villagers take photographs together. We're giddy. We can't believe how terrible we look, plus we're all sure we're going to go into overtime. We're going to make some scratch. The sky darkens and the assistant director assembles our group where the first shot of the night is being set up. He gives us the scoop.

"There's a giant green troll chasing you through the streets. The troll will be CGIed in postproduction later, so for now, you'll see a prop guy carrying a long stick with lights on the top of it. But you're actors, right? You can all pretend to see the troll."

One of the villagers portrayed the grandmother in *Napoleon Dynamite*. Another is a recognizable comedian who once starred in his own Showtime comedy special. "I think we can manage," we murmur amid chuckles.

. . . . . .

There appears to be an army of prop guys readying the area. They hose down the cobblestones with water. My period boots have only a thin leather sole and are soaked through to my tights, but I'm not going to be the first to complain. Horses will run past us, we're told. The magical words "hazard pay" spread through the group in an excited whisper.

"Hazard pay for the horses and the water."

"How much extra do we get?"

"I don't know, but it's a lot!" one of the villagers exclaims.

We are instructed to assemble in front of the director, who makes his selection. "You, you, and you." Including me. These are the only words he will address directly to us during the entire twelve hours we will spend together. The assistant director places we few, we happy few, we band of villagers on the street and the other principals head back to the honey wagon. Grasshopper and Ole Toothless aren't principals, but they get prime spots in the front of the pack. I'm not surprised. These guys look fossilized. I would feature them.

"Who wants to carry a torch?" the prop master barks.

"A lit torch?"

"Yeah."

"Like, on fire?"

"Yeah."

"Me, I want to do that!"

I think of myself as someone who is up for adventure. I've performed roles where I've had explosive charges attached to my person, fired machine guns, learned to sing opera, kissed Rodney

Dangerfield. And just like that, a prop guy dips a heavy wooden club wrapped in gauze into a bucket of kerosene, hands it to me and ignites it with a blowtorch. No one has asked, *Are you someone who should be carrying a torch? Have any suicidal ideation? How well do you balance running on wet cobblestones? Have any anger management issues?* How about wondering what kind of person jumps at the chance to run through the streets with a lit torch? Nope.

"Is there anything we should know about these torches?" I ask casually.

"Oh, we'll do fire training." But as he steps back into the shadows, the shot is called.

"Action. Villagers with torches run toward the troll," I hear the director say from behind a video monitor, where he's viewing a live feed of the footage being shot.

A mob of two dozen peasants rushes forward, jostling for position. Each one of us principals knows that if you aren't recognizable on camera, you will not earn residuals. Each one of the background people knows if they are recognizable, they have a shot at being upgraded to principal. It's clear that no one in charge cares about which of us are seen.

It's been almost thirty years since I worked as background, and that's what this feels like. I was always sure that my talent would catch the eye of the director. Now I'm just trying not to slip and fall.

"Bait the troll with your torches!"

Villagers are thrusting their torches at the imaginary menace.

. . . . . .

"Now turn and run."

As I pivot, something hot brushes the back of my neck.

"Uh, you." He points to the bonneted female extra whose torch is dangerously close to my hair. It's my PTA buddy. "I love your enthusiasm, lady, but we don't carry that much insurance. Hold your torch a little higher." And that's the extent of our fire training. "I can't sell cupcakes at Jazz band B's concert on Friday night if my head goes up in flames," I say, trying to remain friendly, but I catch a glint in her eye that tells me she's vying for a good position. It's every serf for herself, and I'll have to watch my back. We repeat this several times. Each time the director adds and subtracts extras from a seemingly endless supply that emerges from the background tent.

"Did you put mascara back on?" the makeup person shouts over the chaos. She has singled me out between shots. PTA mom is wearing frosted coral lip gloss, another gal has visibly feathered bangs, but something about me just irks her. I actually have put mascara back on.

"No, I didn't."

She swabs more dirt on my face and then pulls out a wimple and pushes it over my hair and low down onto my forehead and retreats to the sidelines. I ask one of the assistant directors if he thinks it will be a continuity problem that I now am wearing a wimple, as I've been established without it. He explodes into peals of laughter. "All of you peasants are, like, this big in the frame," he says, pinching his thumb and forefinger into an inch. Yes, my mascara must certainly be distracting in the infinitesimally miniature pixel it is taking up in the frame of the commercial. I am basically a lumpy sack topped with a doily. On the other hand, it's surprisingly freeing to have any burden of beauty lifted.

After the shot, the production team begins setting up on another part of the street and the principals are dismissed. No one comes to check in on us for the next three hours. It's forty degrees and the sewer smell is so strong that we can't close the door to the honey wagon, so we're shivering. We abandon ship, head into the background tent to warm up, then set off in search of information. We run into a crew guy who is handing out army blankets. We wrap them around ourselves and wander over to an area we can see lit from several hundred feet away. They are shooting another vignette. Only background actors are in the shot. PTA mom is pushing a rusty wheelbarrow piled high with dirt through a cobblestoned alleyway. I make a mental note to let her do all heavy lifting at school functions in the future—she's an ox. We inquire if we are needed and the assistant director stares at us like we've asked him to explain string theory. "We'll call you when we need you."

By one a.m., we're still waiting to hear when we'll be called to the set. One of the villagers tells us that she's done another spot with this director.

She was one of two actresses cast in the same role for that job.

"I like your face, but I like her body better," he told her.

During the shoot, each actress alternately performed the same action, which consisted of loading paper into a copier. They shared a dressing room and were called to set as "Body" and

"Face." Face is incredibly beautiful. She is French, and even though her flawless complexion is stained with dirt, she's fetchingly gamine. Dressed as she is in a low-cut bodice, I can't even imagine how the other actress could have a better body. Months later, she found out that Body had won out. French Face's version never made it out of the can.

"But he casts me a lot. He likes to see my face."

Uh-oh. This makes all of us worried. There are a lot of us villagers. It also hits me that the women villagers basically fit into two categories: maidens and crones. There is nothing in between. In fact, as the median life span of a female serf during the Middle Ages was forty-three, I am actually too old for this job, and I feel very grateful indeed to be here.

At least in a modern setting an actress can hope for age-appropriate roles spanning from girls (with variations on a scale of sluttiness) to mother, MILF, professional, cougar, and then death. If you age with enough gravitas and can carry off serious eyewear, you might fit in a role as a society doyenne or judge somewhere between cougar and death, but like most professions in America, show business has become an all-or-nothing business. Many roles that might have gone to someone like me are regularly offered to and accepted by current and former stars.

Yet there are always a slew of supporting roles for men of a certain age. These craggy gentlemen play anonymous communicators of exposition, relaying forgettable lines of dialogue like *Sir, you're needed in the war room*, or sit stony-faced through tension-filled scenes portraying senior members of the armed forces. With the ban on women serving in armed combat now lifted, an unintended positive consequence will be that future generations of actresses should see more unremarkable but re-munerative employment opportunities. Perhaps the real sign that women have found equal footing in the world will be when we get to see a collection of scowling female Army generals *leaning in* around a conference table in *Iron Man 7.*

By two a.m., we four female villagers have bonded. It's so late there's simply no doing anything productive with our time, like reading or studying for a real estate license, so we're talking to stay awake. Face tells us about her Brigitte Bardot tribute band, her first marriage and how she hopes to have children within the next two years; she's thirty-six, after all. We promise to come and see her perform and even though my son sent me a text earlier in the day putting me on notice that "we don't know each other in cyberspace," I tell her it's worth it to have kids. She should try to get pregnant soon—tonight, if possible. Another actress works in historic preservation and has just been offered an administrative position at a prestigious university in Richmond, Virginia. I look at her dirt-smeared face peering out from under a dull gray wool snood. "You have to take that job," I say. "You have to get out of this town—tonight, if possible," I implore her with an urgency that suggests she's plotting a prison break and I'm going to help her dig the tunnel with spoons. We're each listing our favorite meals like we're kids at summer camp or cellmates on death row. On a typical shoot, you will be given a heads-up on when you'll be needed so you can gauge your energy, but we're in an information void. Every hour or so, we check in with one of the assistant di-rectors, who just shrugs dismissively. We trudge back to our new

. . . . . .

digs, the background tent. We principals are the only ones there; the extras are all on the set. We're starting to lose our connection to the production. We're adrift, grazing at the craft services table on salty chips and nuts out of boredom. One of the villagers begins sipping liquid from a flask he's hidden in his gunnysack, and that's the last we see of him for the rest of the night.

"Screw it," Napoleon Dynamite's grandmother announces. "I'm not gonna force my way into a shot." Snatching the wimple off her head, she heads into one of the compartments to sleep the whole thing off.

By four a.m., our newly appointed chair of the historic preservation department (she emailed her acceptance at three a.m.) is fast asleep, and the remaining male villagers are napping as well. There's only one hour left before sunrise, and French Face and I are the only ones still motivated enough by the prospect of residuals and insurance benefits to keep our eyes open, but even we are fading. I decide it's time to take things into our own hands. I grab my new BFF, Best French Face, and rouse us into action.

"I'm not going to let you miss out on being in another one of this director's commercials. I made an effort to look this terrible. Let's not let this night go to waste."

Cloaked in our blankets, we head out to find the production. The bright klieg lights have moved farther up the street. The set decorators are dressing a town square with fresh bales of hay.

My BFF and I casually drift closer to the video village. I sidle up to a portable heater that's been placed next to the director and pretend to warm my hands, even though it's really my wet feet that are freezing. At the same time, I drop my blanket so the director doesn't forget that I am actually an actor and not one of the dozens of crew people. A crew person in a wimple would be unusual, but I can't take the chance; the clock is ticking. No one bothers to go down to rouse the four other villagers; they will sleep through this last setup, but my BFF and I are in.

We are standing in the town square, our arms laden with baskets of bread, when the giant troll bursts through a wall, bricks tumble down and we run for our lives. My heart is pounding, my eyes dart back and forth, searching for a safe route as I hurry to escape being crushed by that troll. As I sprint, my velvet bodice bursts open. I've snacked on too much salty craft service, but covered as it is with the tunic and shawl, no one notices or cares. Besides, I am merely a tiny bundle of faded fabrics moving across the frame. The sun begins to rise in the distance and I hear the director call, "Cut. It's a wrap."

The air is clear as I drive home. I've survived the night without my head catching on fire. By the time I arrive home it doesn't matter what I do for a living, I'm just happy to have a warm shower. I fall asleep dreaming about the dough I will make when the commercial runs. Dan told me the spot cost millions of dollars. Surely they will run it night and day.

Six months later, the commercial hasn't aired and I receive an update from Dan. The technology this spot is touting turns out not to work. The company has spent millions of dollars filming a commercial for something that's a dud. The agency has determined that hazard pay will not be forthcoming. I will not maraud on national television. It's disappointing enough to make me want to run through the streets with a lit torch. Of course, that's something I might have been able to get away with when I was younger, but at this age I can only do that if a camera is rolling.

AT LEAST I MADE AN EFFORT

> **Dear God,**
>
> **Is it a sin for an atheist to post on both JDate and ChristianMingle?**

"Love. It's the final frontier," the Love Coach declares during our phone call.

"Well, you're the expert," I tell her, "but I thought space was the final frontier."

"Nope, it's love. Women have forgotten how to be feminine. We've lost touch with our sensuality."

I'm interviewing the Love Coach, a professional in the lucrative field of romance, for a women's magazine, but I am suspicious of her enterprise. We take for granted that there have long been baseball and football coaches, but now there are all manner of specialized "experts" who regularly award themselves honorary degrees. *I've earned a doctorate in life!* appears on numerous websites I visit while researching the story.

She tells me that her work is "on the cutting edge of feminism." I live at the intersection of feminism and Feministing, so I take a claim like that seriously. *Are we talking first-, second-, third- or fourth-wave feminism?* I wonder. As I understand it, the first wave gave us the vote, while the second freed us from our kitchens and bras. Postfeminism promised we could have it all. The third wave made sexy bras safe for grrls as long as we're wearing them for our own enjoyment, and the fourth wave promises we can blog about it all. I was raised with second-wave values in a postfeminist world and now find myself surrounded by third- and fourth-wavers. I am easily identifiable as the oldest of the women I share an office with. I'm the only one without tattoos, ironic eyeliner, fluid sexual preferences and a Pinterest account.*

"Do women really need to pay someone to help us with our love lives? Don't we seek out our girlfriends for help?" I ask her.

"I give them a totally objective eye."

She might have a point there. No matter how close you are, there is an unspoken line you cannot cross with even your closest girlfriends. Saying something negative about someone a friend is dating, considering dating or married to, if they're not already halfway through divorce proceedings, can be a friendship ender.

---

*Piercings as well. I am certain there is a wide range of piercings under their clothing, though I've never asked for a visible inspection. Even when these women are fifty, there will be forty-year-olds who look visibly different from them—they will probably be tattoo-free.

Also, they don't listen. "Do you think that Jamie might be gay?" every single one of my friends had suggested to me during the six months he and I dated. Nothing—not his gender-neutral name, his lilting voice, sex that I could only describe as All That Pounding, nor the dresses and wigs in his closet— could convince me. "Some people take Halloween very seriously." I shrugged. It wasn't until he broke up with me to date someone named Todd that I conceded they might have a point.

"You need to stay current with online dating etiquette," she tells me. "I continually do research, and that's one of the things we'll focus on in this weekend's Magical Mani-festing Makeover. See you bright and early tomorrow."

Magical Mani-festing Makeover. It's hard to imagine how this workshop will have anything to do with the cutting edge of anything other than the razor I'll want to slit my wrists with. I'm not sure which of those words is most frightening to me, or if it's the combination of the three, even though I have heard about the inexplicable vagaries of online dating from my girlfriends who are in their forties or fifties and newcomers to it. My fifty-one-year-old friend Denise was just matched with two people by one of the most popular fee-based sites: her brother and a homeless guy who goes by the name Bling-Bling.

Seven of the Love Coach's clients are flying in for this workshop and are scheduled for a wardrobe revamp with a professional stylist in the morning. As part of my assignment, I will observe their shopping expedition. Who knows? Maybe these women suffer from some terrible afflictions that they need ministering to: clubfoot, harelip, hirsutism?

. . . . . .

The next day, I am the first of our group to arrive at a local boutique.

I have planted myself on a low velvet settee when the manager of the store greets me. She looks to be about my age but has been improbably squeezed into skin-hugging jeans and a low-cut denim bustier mostly untied with leather lacing. It's more sausage casing than clothing. The glare from her lip gloss is blinding. "You want things that have some va-va-voom, right?" She thinks I am part of the Love Coach's team and I'm not sure if LC's told anyone I am a writer or I'm supposed to be her assistant. I don't want to blow my cover, so I say, "Sure," and head to the racks of clothing.

The dresses look like bedazzled napkins. I unearth a few items that I might consider wearing, like a tailored white shirt and slim black pants, when the Love Coach wafts in decked out in towering stilettos and a slinky aubergine sheath. She's wearing a scent she's created called Vulvacious. It has a lingering sweet smell that clings to the air around her. It's a Proustian combination of bubble gum and vagina. She's accompanied by someone I intuit to be her stylist. He's emaciated, wearing a pinstriped suit with a vest and is carrying the Love Coach's Shih Tzu. He takes one look at my selections: "These ladies are going on dates, they're not preparing tax returns," and begins pulling out sheer halter tops and shiny spandex jeans, a look I'll call "stripper casual." Is this what women are supposed to wear for a date? Is this what *I* should be wearing on dates with my husband? I actually can't remember the last time my husband and I went on a date, but I am absolutely certain I didn't make this kind of effort to look sexy. I'm not sure

. . . . . .

I ever have in my entire life, but then I haven't been single in al-most two decades.

I want to be helpful, so I grab everything I can find with a plunging neckline. As if on cue, the clients arrive and it's far, far worse than I anticipated. The women are uniformly friendly, at-tractive and intelligent. They've flown in from across the globe, including locations as diverse as Morocco, Detroit, Texas, Vir-ginia and Saskatchewan. They are all approximately my age. I would have felt so much better about this makeover if just one of them had at least a social anxiety disorder, if not leprosy. I zip and unzip them and suggest accessories. I pull the stylist aside. "Do they need to look so . . . tarty?" He looks at me like I've suggested that these ladies enlist in the North Korean People's Army. "Peo-ple like to get dressed up on dates," he says flatly, adding, "many of us get stuck with a look left over from the last time we felt really attractive, which might have been when we were in high school." I nod and try to move away without him noticing the scrunchy that's anchoring my ponytail.

The stylist and LC insist on higher heels, more cleavage and more color. More pink! I was never a girly girl. I never wanted to ride a pony or be a princess. I've always been pink-averse and ever since Victoria's Secret began targeting teenage girls with their Love Pink campaign, I've found the shade particularly loathsome.* Nevertheless, LC insists on pinks of all configura-

---

*The pink ribbon campaign to promote breast cancer awareness lost any credibility it might have had when KFC introduced the pink bucket, despite the fact that their chicken has been known to contain PhIP, a carcinogenic chemical linked to causing breast cancer.

tions: Tufted pink. Ruffled pink. Ruched pink. I feel like I am from an entirely different species from another planet. *Homo crone* from Planet Dowdy.

Armed with their new dating wardrobes, the clients, LC and I caravan to a hotel for the next phase of the makeover. It's a swanky place where electronic dance music pulses in the lobby twenty-four hours a day. Strolling through the lobby I notice the restaurant has morphed into the kind of date-night eatery where you can expect to be served a selection of spicy olives as an entrée. Many years ago, when it was a midpriced establishment, my husband treated us to dinner and an anniversary overnight stay there. The median age in the hotel now appears to be between twenty-five and twenty-five and a half. I hurry into an elevator to avoid being carded. There might actually be an age maximum.

At the rooftop pool area, I can't help but feel like I'm watching meat being carefully packaged as the Love Coach oversees a team that includes a hair and makeup artist and a photographer who snaps candid shots for use on dating sites. Is this cheating? Or is the privilege/punishment of age having the good sense to make sure that you present yourself in the best light possible?

LC catches my eye and pulls me aside. She shows me her clients' "before" photos. There is a preponderance of poufy hair, some unflattering angles and attempts to convey uniqueness that are somehow getting lost in translation. One gal, a nurse practitioner from Texas with symmetrical features, has placed herself behind a sheer curtain of fabric. The image was probably meant to foster an air of mystery; instead, it sends one of two confusing messages: *I have terrible skin and must not be seen with the naked eye*, or *I long to be recruited into a Saudi Arabian harem*. Another client appears to be in her kitchen, preparing a meal with an adult son. Here the intent must have been *I'm a nurturing person*, but the photo screams *We're a package deal*. LC's marketing background is brought home when she points out that most women are dressed in black, while research shows that bright color can positively influence purchasing outcomes, and though I am hesitant to compare this process to purchasing, when I view one "after" photograph, I can see that a hot pink cami really does make you stand out.

Why should I be surprised that people want to game the system? At this very moment, or at any moment, there is a picture of me on my social media feeds that I have taken on a day when I've had my makeup done professionally, rushed home and, before I've scrubbed my face of the multiple layers of flattering war paint, posed in front of my computer camera a minimum of twenty times before picking the shot that I think looks most uncontrived. Even so, I am finding it impossible to look good in a photograph at this age.

All the tricks I honed as an actress don't work anymore. I used to narrow my glance just slightly in what I considered my come-hither look, but I have so little eye left that I just look like I've misplaced one of my several pairs of reading glasses. My lips slightly parted once conveyed a certain wantonness; now it just makes me look parched. A closed, pursed mouth betrayed a touch of defiant insouciance, but now that expression settles into scowling resignation. Can't look down, ever. Too jowly. You must always be smiling in photos when you're fifty, otherwise you look disgruntled, but don't smile *too* much—too many wrinkles.

I thought I'd perfected at least one potentially flattering look—gleeful surprise. This astonishment must be judiciously deployed, as when you're checking out in the grocery line, going through security at an airport, or delivering meals to a sick friend, as it can be puzzling if not traumatizing for others to be subjected to this look. On a positive note, while volunteering at my son's school I have received tutorials from well-meaning committee mothers on everything from how to write a letter and how to check names off a list to how to use double-stick tape, all of which are perfectly appropriate occasions for the astonished look. Poolside with the Love Coach, however, the lighting is so superior, these ladies can't help but look astonishingly gorgeous.

After the photos are all taken, we gather in a suite. Chairs have been positioned in a circle and journals embossed with the words "Love Notes" have been provided for us.

"Put some tissues out," LC whispers to me. "Someone always cries.

"I want you to write down your favorite weather, colors, objects, flower, material, or magical creature," she instructs the group. "These 'essence words' will become user names for your online dating. They will announce to the world who you are so you can attract your perfect mate." She instructs me to do the exercise as an experiment.

"Can Christopher Hitchens be my magical creature?" I say.

"No, it should be iconic."

. . . . . .

"He was pretty iconic."

"A Greek god, a phoenix, a mythical being, you know, the subject of your fantasies."

At this point in my life, I find stainless steel kitchen appliances a turn-on and daydream of being able to afford long-term-care insurance. The best I can come up with is Sun Shower Unicorn. I sound like a Renaissance Pleasure Faire reenactor on acid. Every other combination I can think of makes me sound like a wrestler with a weak bladder. "Platinum Fog." "Steel Rain." "Titanium Thunder."

I want to be useful to the group, so I suggest that the leggy real estate magnate from Morocco should be "Successful and Statuesque." "It needs to be intriguing," corrects LC, who proceeds to brainstorm something so perfect and captivating that I am stopped in my tracks: "Golden Lotus." It really fits her. Impressive. Drawing a blank, I toss out the worst moniker I can dream up, "Green Boots," and all the ladies agree that I radiate "Green Boots." I have no idea if this is a good thing, I suspect it's not, but for the rest of the night, I answer to "Green Boots."

Next, she wants us to pen our most passionate fantasy. "We're taking a stand for love in an age that's increasingly cynical. We're casting our 'love spells.' You can't manifest something unless you declare what you want." I'm manifesting a lot of eye-rolling.

"Do it, Green Boots," Coach orders me.

I feel like a low-rent romance novelist, but I compose a scenario that involves Umberto Eco, Paris and Pinot Noir. I call my composition "Semiotic and Erotic."

. . . . . .

After I read it aloud, I announce, "I've stopped devoting energy to my marriage." I'm first in the group to cry. I am, it turns out, the exact woman the Love Coach described to me on the phone.

Each woman reads what she's written and aside from the fact that the majority of the scenes take place in Paris or on a beach and involve consuming wine or brunch or both, they are all sincerely heartfelt. Texas describes sharing a particularly flavorful egg dish and chokes up. "It's just been so long since I've been intimate with anyone." She says between sobs, "I don't know if I'll ever meet anyone." Love Coach consoles her by allowing that she's really doing this exercise to get to know herself better and that's what matters most.

As I drive home, bottle of Vulvacious in tow, I'm forced to rethink my initial judgment. Has this whole Magical Mani-festing Makeover been one big bait and switch? I am tempted to label it "lip gloss feminism." I am awed by the courage it took for her clients to display so much vulnerability and terrified that I will soon be in their stilettos, conjuring my "love spell" and composing my JDate profile under LC's tutelage if I don't step it up in my marriage.

I decide to skip the second day of the workshop. I've got enough material for my story. Instead, I stop in at a local lingerie outlet near my home. I purchase lacy boy shorts, and bras that have ornate straps and little bows. I gamely try them on for my husband in the afternoon and before I can even douse myself with my new perfume, he tells me he doesn't consider them lingerie. If it's not a garter belt, it doesn't count in his book.

. . . . . .

At Least I Made an Effort

I resent the garter belt. It acts like a framing device for the exact area of my body that I now dislike. Having always been one good poop away from a flat stomach, I'd taken for granted the easy gait of the very slim. I've heard middle-aged thickness described as a swim floatie, but that sounds too buoyant to me. I liken it to always having a sweater wrapped around my waist. Ironically, the last time I regularly draped something over my hips was when I first got my period. I spent the entire eighth grade saddled with sweaters because I couldn't remember to bring tampons to school.* I would find it preferable to have the area formerly known as my waist tattooed an attractive and slimming shade, maybe even pink.

At least I made an effort, I repeat to myself, as I catalogue my marriage pros and cons and change back into my Spanx. It should really be called a cons and pros list because when you reach the point of needing a list, the cons come so easily to mind.

Much of our communication in the last few years is down to texts regarding "scheduling," which might be the most unappealing word in the dictionary, next to the phrase "Can we talk?" *Can we talk about scheduling?* A double bummer. My husband has asked me to stop using that phrase, but it's hard to avoid. We've got our own version of Words with Friends. I call it Words with Spouses. I've asked him to stop using "micromanaging" and "agitating." My husband has banned my use of the adjective "delish" and the phrase "I'm sorry you feel that way." Much of the time

---

*And this was in Florida! No one told me that nothing is certain except death, taxes, and back fat.

. . . . . .

we text "whr r u?" "hm" or "wrkng" to each other. Extraneous vowels have disappeared. When we lose consonants, what will be left for us?

Mail-ordered shoes arrive at our doorstep every week. They are inevitably blue oxfords. Sometimes the stitching is visible, sometimes the bottoms are leather, sometimes it's whatever a sole is when it's not leather. They all look the same to me. However, if I speak this sentiment out loud it is very upsetting to him, so I must moderate and add variety to any opinions.

"Those? Too . . . preppy. These? Too . . . sartorial."

"Those are exactly the same pair, just in different sizes."

"Of course, silly! I knew that, I was just testing to see if you were listening to me." When I close my eyes at night, I see a long chain of blue oxfords speeding toward our home.

Books on World War II have also begun showing up at our house at an alarming rate. Since we began dating, he's joked about his father's fascination with Nazi Germany and marveled at the number of books his dad accumulated on the subject. As my husband inches toward fifty himself, I catch him devouring one tome after another late into each night. We always wondered how it started with his dad. Now I know. Where will it end? We all know the answer: a DVR overloaded with History Channel documentaries.

Socks lie abandoned next to the bed. Also next to the bathtub, under the couch and next to our front door. Men slough off socks like snakes shed their skin. There was a period of three months when I took Polaroids of sock clusters wherever I saw them and left the pictures as reminders on the pillow on his side of the bed.

. . . .

The worst part of this was realizing I had become the kind of person who takes pictures of socks, and my husband had witnessed that.

These are small, petty, first-world problems, but such is the stuff of daily life. A few years back, my mother-in-law sent me a copy of *Don't Sweat the Small Stuff.* I've never picked it up except to propel it past my husband's head, but the subtitle really says it all—*And It's All Small Stuff.* It's just that you end up with so much stuff. Our stuff has its *own* stuff.

So many friends our age are in marriages that are failing.

"Are we the last ones standing?" I ask my husband.

"Or running."

We might be.

"Did you hear about David and Michelle splitting up?" he asks me.

"No, really?" I say. "Do you remember the speech he gave at her birthday party? The way he beamed at her, calling her the love of his life?" I was so envious of them that day. "She keeps their linens in a long glass cabinet in the upstairs hallway. I can't even imagine how labor-intensive it is to keep them folded so neatly that you can keep them on display like that. She must have a team of people running that household. Between the linens, her three gorgeous kids and her six-figure salary? It's intimidating."

"She's already got a boyfriend."

"Wow, another reason to envy her. Did you hear about Lucinda and Mark?"

"I saw that one coming."

"I didn't. Don't say anything, they haven't told their kids yet."

. . . . . .

Then there's Gary and Suzanne, and Valentina and Francesca. Both couples are examples of what's been recently termed by economists as "sleeping with the enemy." They're stuck in underwater mortgages and can't afford to separate. It's not a stretch to say that every time we hear about another marriage biting the dust we experience it as both a loss and a wish fulfillment.

My husband and I might be approaching a big window of opportunity. Our empty nest would seem to be within sight. The classic scenario for so many of my generation was for parents to split when the kids left home. My husband's parents separated when he was in college.

"Next year we'll have been married one year longer than my parents," my husband announces as we cross paths before we head our separate ways, he to yet more ESPN and me to bed.

"Well, that still gives us time to divorce," I call after him.

Of course, my mother-in-law was in her thirties, with an entire youthful life ahead of her, and I'll be fifty-four when our son graduates high school. Just as daunting an idea as "until death do us part" is what's being called the boomerang effect. Unemployed or underemployed adult children are moving back home after college, so if we're waiting until our kid leaves home to sell our house and call it quits, we might be looking at an additional five years—if we're lucky!

In my own family, an old-world tradition of prolonging misery has been maintained and few have divorced. Thankfully, many have been rescued from long-term suffering by early mortality. Previous generations with their shorter life spans never

· · · · · ·

anticipated marriages would last this long. I lie awake wondering what new revelations will occur with our longer life spans, making age—not love, not space—the final frontier.

At the wedding of the first of my classmates' children to get married, I inadvertently share a bit of hard-won wisdom. During the celebratory luncheon, the twenty-three-year-old groom, whose diapers I have changed, was speaking of how wonderful it is that he can fully reveal himself to his bride when "Oh my God, that's a terrible idea—don't do that, Zachary!" slips right out of my mouth before I can stop it with a swig of wine.*

There are things in life that are really best experienced alone. Using a toothpick, sex, and longtime marriage are often most satisfying when you are separated from others by many miles. I had that experience on the night I ran away from home. I can't remember what it was that sent me packing. It probably involved the word "scheduling." But on this night, I had the Love Coach's number in my back pocket; I spritzed myself with Vulvacious for good measure and headed to my friend Marin's place.

Marin left her husband after he had one too many indiscretions with women from their church marital counseling group, although she acknowledges her marriage had been over for years. She says it was like she finally lost that last 235 pounds she was

---

*A lot of research has come out recently about teenagers' tendency to overestimate their future potential. Perhaps this optimism is needed in order to further the species. Which is why it also makes sense not to share too much about childbirth and aging with people so far from the experience that it would be too frightening for them to keep calm and carry on.

. . . . . .

lugging around. Since then, she's remade her life: she's never looked better, has established a new career after years of being out of the job force in one of history's worst economies and has even joined a new church. Marin has two kids, one an athletic boy and the other a girl the same age as my son. In fact, they were playmates as toddlers. This beautiful girl scores high on the autism spectrum. Lovely to look at, she has few social graces and attends a specialized education program. It's doubtful she will ever live on her own or hold any form of employment. She stalks the house like a cheetah.

My friend is indefatigable. How much caffeine and Klonopin would it take for me to be as relentlessly upbeat and resourceful if I divorced at this point in my life?

I arrive at her home at around seven p.m. A huge Rottweiler greets me at the door. His name is Buster or Bruiser or Butch, he weighs more than my kid, has a bandanna around his neck and it turns out I will be sharing a room with him. He belongs to a twenty-five-year-old student with whom Marin trades housing for babysitting duties. The student is spending the night at a boyfriend's house. The dog immediately begins licking my face and neck. "He must really like you," Marin says. Wow, that Love Coach is good; even male dogs respond to Vulvacious.

After the kids are ensconced in their bedrooms for the night, the doorbell rings and it's one of Marin's ex's exes, who has become a close friend. They have a standing date once a week to review men who've responded to their ads on an over-forty dating site. I have to get a look, as this could soon be my life. Marin pours from her selection of airplane wines.

. . . . . .

At Least I Made an Effort

The men who have responded to Marin's ad would appear to be in the same general range of men the Love Coach's clients, the ex, and I might be interested in.

All the candidates appear to be professionals of some sort and claim to be between the ages of forty-five and fifty-five, so they're probably fifty to sixty at the very least. Two-thirds of them are posed next to fireplaces with glasses of wine in their hands. That seems to be a good thing, an image that communicates *I am a real person, a stable man with a home that has a hearth, or at least I have access to a hearth. I know how to relax and have a glass of wine.* The other third have taken some creative license with their profiles. One sunburned gentleman is pictured on a boat with a beer in his hand and the rest of a six-pack within arm's reach. I studied just enough semiotics in college to know that if I analyzed this photo long enough, I might come to the conclusion that this man was a loner, a drinker prone to disappearing on lost weekends. Too Hemingway. I wouldn't date him. Another is at the beach. He is wearing leather sandals. "Too much man foot!" Marin's friend announces, and we nod our heads in unison. No one wants to see man foot in a picture. He's also wearing shorts and a fanny pack. How often is this guy in shorts? Might he show up for a date in shorts? Photos of men that have long hair scream *romance novel, Def Leppard tribute band member,* or *might have a long pinky fingernail.* What if some of these candidates are clients of a male love coach and these photos are professionally staged? This thought is frankly bewildering.

As we page through the profiles, the most unsatisfying part of

. . . . . .

evaluating potential companions is that each person is pictured solo. It makes sense that your friends and family might not want their photos included on a dating site, but this makes for thousands of single people presented out of context. "You are the company you keep" is an adage that seems particularly true when you're nearing fifty. Each headshot announces, *I AM ALONE*. It takes only a short leap of the imagination to picture any of these men conversing with a volleyball that has a face painted on it, which they've named Wilson.*

The whole online dating world appears to be a reductive way of learning about people, yet there might be some advantages. I didn't know until long after I married my husband that he had lived under the illusion that he might have had a career in major-league baseball if only his mother hadn't discouraged him. It just never came up. Perhaps if I had met him online, I might have spotted his large collection of baseball caps in the background of a picture of him in front of a fireplace. That actually would have been helpful; at least I wouldn't have been surprised by the long hours of ESPN viewing he's racked up. And yet, among the three of us, we know at least a dozen friends who've found rewarding relationships online, so we flag three or four guys who are wearing long pants and have open smiles for follow-up. (Marin instituted this criteria after a particularly harrowing experience; when you can't see the teeth, it might be because there are none.)

---

*If I ran a dating service, I would require notarized tributes from at least two friends who've never been convicted of felonies from each candidate in the database.

. . . . . .

Six months from now, one of us could be sharing a glass of wine in front of one of those hearths.

Marin shows me to the babysitter's room and Barker or Boomer or whatever the gigantic canine's name is rouses himself long enough to jump on the bed. He buries his nose in my neck and pants loudly while I try to fall asleep. *At least he's not snoring,* I tell myself.

I lie awake most of the night wondering how Green Boots would fare on FarmersOnly.com. I never asked how much the Love Coach charges for her services, and I definitely haven't allowed for romance consultation in any what-if-we-get-divorced budgets. I bet she's pricey; she's got that little teacup breed—they can be high-strung and sometimes need therapy. I wake up early in the morning in a sweat remembering how one erstwhile dater, touting his sense of humor, had included a joke on his profile page. *Why did the squirrel swim across the river on his back? To keep his little nuts dry!* I quickly and quietly pack my overnight bag and head home.

I hear my husband in the kitchen making breakfast for our son as I walk through the front door. "Just went for an early run," I fib to our kid. I offer to take over, but Jeff says he's got it covered and he'll drive the carpool.

"Mom, you smell good," my son calls out to me. "You smell like . . ."

"Bubble gum. I know. Thanks!" I say as I head upstairs to our bedroom. I'm exhausted from my sleepless night.

As I undress, I notice there's a computer on my husband's side of the bed. I glance at the screen and see a story he's writing. It's about how he chooses not to see the effects aging is having on my lower torso by pixelating his vision when he looks at my posterior. It never occurred to me that when he tells me how great I still look, he might also be "making an effort." This is quite simply one of the kindest gestures I've been treated to in my life.

My husband comes in the bedroom and whispers he's sorry. I lie down and he places a throw around my body and I marvel at his ability to tuck the covers around my backside while simultaneously blurring his vision.

"Did you think marriage would be like this?" I ask.

"I thought there'd be more fucking," he replies.

"I thought there'd be more money," I say, and I realize my gynecologist was right in advising me to stay funny. Maintaining a sense of humor is the final frontier or at least our saving grace as we age.

"What's that great scent?" he asks. "It's like . . ."

"Vagina?"

"Yes. Mmm . . ." He inhales deeply and nuzzles my neck. I decide he really doesn't need to know that the very same spot was occupied until thirty minutes ago by an amorous Rottweiler.

He heads out and it occurs to me that maybe his story was intended to be a metaphor. Is he saying that he chooses to gloss over what's come behind? He's witnessed my bad behavior, crappy career decisions, poor housekeeping skills and yet he doesn't focus on it. Now, that would be very, very clever and shockingly compassionate.

Before closing my eyes, I catch sight of our two ginger cats

. . . . . .

contentedly slumbering in a wicker basket at the foot of our bed. I brought these two into our home because my husband was beside himself with grief after our beloved twenty-one-year-old cat's exit from this earthly litter box. The kittens had been abandoned by their mother, so we bottle-fed them. Now my husband is so completely bonded to these animals, I wouldn't be surprised to come home one day and find him "wearing" them in an infant carrier.

The cats, now a year old, have outgrown this basket they shared as kittens but refuse to give it up. They sleep stacked on top of each other. Are we becoming those ginger cats?

I'm going to keep the Love Coach on my speed dial. My garter belt days might be behind me, but a sexy slip, maybe even pink, might be in my future. At least I can say I made an effort.

THIS IS FIFTY

Int. a Bedroom in
Los Angeles—Late at Night

It's not the suburban Los Angeles bedroom you've seen in romantic comedies like *Knocked Up* or *This Is 40*. This bedroom didn't have a set designer. It's not designed. It's furnished.

The furniture, including a makeup vanity, armoire and set of drawers, is from the Art Deco period, the combined effect almost achieving the look that was once referred to as "shabby chic," a trademark style that emphasizes the allure of timeworn objects, though in this case it's a bit more shabby than chic. In just the right light, it might resemble a modest Parisian hotel room in an outer arrondissement, but in full sunlight it's more akin to a B and B outside Fresno, raisin capital of the world. An upholstered armchair that looks as though a pack of lions has been sharpening their claws on it sits next to an unused cat scratching post.

This Is Fifty

CLOSE ON: Five different TV remotes piled on a leather ottoman at the foot of the bed. One for the TV, one for the DVD player, one for the cable, one for a VCR that hasn't been in use since 2001, and one belonging to a laser disc player, a technology that never really took. Each of the occupants suspects there might be a slim possibility that the signal from one of these remotes is doing something that makes the entire system work. It would sound cliché to note that three out of the five devices are flashing 12:00, but you know they are. The VCR simply reads: —:—.

CAMERA PANS ACROSS the foot of the bed.

A large comfy looking California king dominates the room. A closer look reveals what appears to be a line down the middle of the bed. It is actually where two comforters meet. Each side has its own blanket.

CLOSE ON: Her nightstand. We see a plastic night guard container, a pair of tweezers, a jumbo-sized half-empty bottle of over-the-counter acid reflux medication. The top is gone, having been misplaced during the mad rush to get the bottle open. An assortment of reading that includes: *You Can't Sell Your Teenager on eBay, So Don't Even Think About It*; *The Blue Zone Diet—Eating Your Way to a Longer Life*; *Anger Management for Couples—Yes, You Need it, Too, Not Just Your Partner.* Two pairs of reading glasses resting next to each other. A package of AA batteries.

. . . . . .

I See You Made an Effort

OPEN WIDER TO REVEAL: His nightstand. History books.
Nazi: A New History of the Third Reich; *Nazi: A New History of the Third Reich, Part II*; and *How the Third Reich Has Been Reinterpreted in New Historical Accounts*. A small pyramid of crumpled receipts, an open box of Breathe Right strips and two pairs of reading glasses.

A Teenage Boy enters the bedroom to speak to his Mother.

The Mother is reading her dog-eared copy of You Can't Sell Your Teenager on eBay.

SON

Mom, I need a poster board and markers for my science project.

MOTHER

We'll pick up something tomorrow.

SON

It's due tomorrow.

MOTHER

Are you kidding me? It's nine p.m. How many times have we talked about not starting projects the night before they're due? You know, if I were really a good parent I would let you fail, because that's the

only way you're going to learn to be more
organized.

*She closes the book, takes off her glasses and opens the
drawer to her nightstand. She reaches her hand inside,
intending to put them away.*

MOTHER (CONT'D.)
I don't even know if there's anything open this time
of night. I'm going to tell your dad . . .

*We hear the unmistakable whirring and thumping sound
of a vibrator that has accidentally been turned on.*

Both the Mother and the Son freeze.

She switches it off as quickly as she can.

SON
Mom!!!

MOTHER
Oh my God!!!

*In that moment, she knows that he knows what that sound is
and he knows that she knows that he knows.*

. . . . . .

SON

Mom.

Shaking his head, he turns and exits the bedroom.

MOTHER

I am so sorry.

She calls to the Husband, who is in the bathroom adjoining the bedroom.

MOTHER (CONT'D.)

Honey, how much money have we saved for family counseling?

HUSBAND (*calling from the bathroom*)

None.

MOTHER (*calling after the son*)

I am so sorry!!!!

FADE TO GRAY

. . . . . .

HOLLYWOOD ADJACENT

> *Dear God,*
>
> *L.A. is a great big freeway. The weeks really did turn into years.*

I'm going shopping with one of my best friends and I am terrified.

He and I have known each other for twenty years. We met acting in an independent film that never saw the light of day. There's a saying in show business that when a project is a hit, everyone involved ends up hating each other, but failures have their own unique bonding power. It's true. It's like you made it off the *Titanic* on the same lifeboat.

The project we did together was poorly written and disastrously executed. The producer and director had been romantically involved but stopped speaking to each other during the first three hours of shooting and spent the remaining three weeks passing hostile messages back and forth through the cast members. The makeup artists were endearing drag queens, but as they frequented a local dance club every night, they didn't show up until long after the first scenes of the day had been shot. In addition, the director of photography was not only toiling on our film but also working hard on maintaining a toxically high blood alcohol level. Once he showed up with his arm in a sling from putting it through a glass window the previous night. "Don't ask," he said when he came to work with a patch over one eye. We didn't.

Many actors are fortunate enough to travel the world. Michael Caine has said he often signed on to films for their exotic locations. Hence, *Blame It on Rio*. I've found myself more often than not in a dilapidated warehouse in Pacoima with a view of a cement factory.

This film was shot in a small town in Georgia that had the highest per capita number of serial killers in the nation at that time. Only three people died while we were there, but they were all in the same family, so technically they don't count in serial-murder statistics. The budget was so low and the shooting days so long that my friend and I not only shared a dressing room, we also napped on the same twin bed, at the same time. The filmmakers ran out of money three-quarters of the way through the shoot. Conveniently, there was an "electrical fire," which burned down the house we were using as a location. This happy accident resulted in a six-figure insurance settlement that meant we could reshoot numerous scenes on a soundstage at a higher budget. Still, the film turned out to be a complete turd. Stories from that gig are a perennial source of fun for my friend and me, particularly now that it's in the rearview mirror.

. . . . . .

Our friendship has survived because we dated for the briefest interlude, during which time both of us recognized that we were better friends than lovers. At first, I enjoyed the novelty of his insistence that I feign unconsciousness or English as a second language during sex. Once, when he was in a play, he asked me to come over and wash his clothes because "Hamlet doesn't do laundry!" But the night he warily inquired if he really needed to tell people we were dating at the party we were heading to, I answered, "No, you don't, because we aren't anymore." I found men who were happy to converse with me and he found women who were willing to do his laundry.

At that time, we were at relatively the same place in our careers. We were both young enough to have a seemingly endless number of opportunities and goodwill directed our way. As an actor, I have gone on to some remunerative gigs, but I've had my share of dry spells, flops and terrible career moves. I've also been blessed with an innate inability to recognize entertainment destined for mainstream popularity. I read for a role on *Friends* and was subsequently invited to attend the taping of the pilot. "This'll never last," I announced to everyone within earshot.*

Not my pal. He has been continuously employed on one television series or another and has invested well, so, as he puts it, "Money is no longer an issue." He owns several homes and employs numerous assistants who each have their own assistants, all of whom have walkie-talkies. He travels with a bodyguard and

---

*I also anticipated that the Tea Party, the word "synergy," and the popularity of kale would be passing fascinations.

. . . . . .

his child has two nannies who also have walkie-talkies. His income supports a community the size of a small Pacific Island nation, so it only makes sense that he has a legion of seemingly well-compensated and readily available staff members.

That our friendship has endured can also be chalked up to our having met before the tsunami of money and adulation overtook his daily life. We have seen each other through turbulent emotional times. We know where the bodies are buried. But between his work, his extensive vacation schedule and that he's taken up flying, there are few times and places on this earth when we are in the same city at the same time.

He's asked for my help in picking out a birthday present for his wife. I actually had planned to do some shopping myself as well, but not at the expensive boutique he has picked, which has so few items on display, it's like they are exotic animals in a private zoo. Still, it seemed like a perfect opportunity to get together.

The ex-boyfriend encounter is the most difficult occasion to dress for. Your appearance must communicate *I am doing just fine without you, even better than I was when I was with you; in fact, your approval means so little I dressed in under a minute.* Nothing is as strenuous as effortlessness, so I'm already running late when an email lands in my in-box informing me that the $8,800 I was expecting to receive in theatrical royalties was incorrectly calculated using numbers applicable to a different scale production, which means I will be receiving less than a fourth of the fee. Coincidentally, I spent that identical sum on my son's braces and music lessons just this week. I check in twice with my

. . . . . .

attorney to see if there's been a mistake, even though I know each and every time my attorney opens an email it costs me even more money, but I can't stop myself. This sum is a significant part of my income this year and I experience the loss like a sharp blow to the stomach.

I will go shopping anyway, I tell myself. My ability to roll with the punches proves that I am not defined by the vagaries of my finances. I don't measure my worth by the numbers in my bank account. I am not going to let this keep me from this much-anticipated get-together with my friend. I genuinely enjoy his company, plus, to be the confidante of the superfamous is a privilege that confers a sense of importance on the receiver. It's the Hollywood equivalent of being granted an audience with the Pope and having the Holy See enlist your advice with his moral compass. Still, the famous come with their own set of rules.

"You're late," he notes when I arrive twenty minutes past the appointed time. They can keep you waiting, but you can't be late for the über-famous. I am tempted to tell him that my son was hit by a bus just to see his reaction, but I'm not that good an actress.

I don't want to admit to how much care went into looking this casual, and if I say too much about my financial woes it might make him feel responsible for me, and if I were to actually verbalize the difference in our status it would be awkward and might even threaten our ability to continue our friendship. The reality of making a living as a freelancer has become such a remote and distant memory, I know he would be surprised to learn that I've

. . . . . .

been collecting unemployment benefits, but I must avoid being viewed as a burden.*

"I am so sorry, traffic was worse than usual. The 405 Freeway was closed for Carmaggedon."†

"Oh yeah, it's a bitch." He nods in agreement. "When we had construction near us, I didn't leave my house for a week." Traffic is one of the few equalizers in Los Angeles. In Los Angeles, commiserating over traffic is conducted with the same solemnity as the lack of transparency in totalitarian dictatorships is debated elsewhere around the globe.

And it's time to go shopping. He's already treating his wife and her extended family to an Italian vacation, but he wants to surprise her with a small token of his affection as well.

"A purse," I say. "She'd never expect that from you," and for some reason, I am suddenly energized. I am speaking with so much enthusiasm you would think I had invented purses or bought stock when the idea was first thought up. Such is the thrill that the anticipation of spending large sums of cash can create.

I have never spent more than $200 on a handbag. The only way I'd pay $10,000 for a bag is if it contained $9,750 in cash and gave me a hot-stone massage. I have never stepped into the luxury purse section of a department store, and it's like I am crossing

---

*Most of the people who hit the jackpot in Hollywood, if not everywhere, end up with a long list of family members to support: ne'er-do-well cousins, siblings who live in trailer parks and ex-spouses with large monthly overheads. They don't need their friends to be on the gravy train; that's why the famous seek out other, equally famous folks for friendship.

†Only in L.A. would a freeway closure receive a nickname that connotes the end of the world!

the border into another country. I don't have a passport, but my friend is my temporary visa. I have always considered these over-priced lady trophies gauche, but approaching the sleek, modular vessels enclosed in temperature-controlled glass casing, I can feel their power.

In the late nineties I frequently purchased knockoff Birkin bags from Ousmane, a friendly Senegalese gentleman who stood on the corner of Amsterdam and Seventy-Seventh street in Man-hattan. I bought them not only for myself but also for my friends. That ended when Gail Collins wrote about a supposed al-Qaeda connection to the knockoff handbag trade. Looking back now, it seems unlikely anyone would go to the trouble to manufacture, ship and sell faux designer bags to buy bombs when you could just drop a shipment of Hermès on us; even the fakes are really heavy

I am carrying a well-worn satchel fashioned out of a recycled plastic tarp. My bag has a shoulder strap made from a seat belt. I'm sure that the salespeople assume I am his assistant.

I spot a purse that seems like it might be perfect. It's a boxy black leather bag, large and rather unassuming. It has an under-stated elegance. It also has a price tag of $20,000. Which is $12,000 more than the amount I thought I was making this month and $18,000 more than what I will receive after I anxiously check my mailbox seven or eight times a day for three weeks. Even my friend admits, "It's outrageous," and I am strangely re-lieved to see there is a limit. I pick out a puffy caramel-colored tote. I inquire if I may touch it and find the texture soft and creamy. It's like butter. I'm tempted to bite into it. It's also so pil-lowy that just stroking it makes me feel sleepy and I am tempted to lay my head down on it. But I hold myself back, because this brioche-shaped bag has a price tag of $6,000, and I can't afford to risk drooling on it.

"It's a keeper," I announce with relish, exercising an executive decision with my companion's credit card.

"You know, if you really want to make this perfect, add in a two-thousand-dollar gift certificate to the store; everyone loves those. I got one once and it was the nicest thing I've ever been given."

Why did I add that caveat? I was given a beautiful if modest antique diamond ring by my husband, and the kisses and hugs I received from my son when he was little were the greatest rewards I could ever hope for in this lifetime, but my heart is racing with anticipation. Am I going to get one as well? I want to be that person, perhaps the only one in his life, who doesn't ask things from him, but I also really, really, especially after my financial news today, really want a nice present and I know he is my only chance at receiving something extravagant.

I simply can't walk out without buying something. Peer pressure. I head off to purchase a birthday gift for my mother. I had intended on purchasing her a travel kit I saw advertised on sale at The Body Shop, consisting of eight bath gels, but instead I fork over $42.50 for a candle. I come back to find he's purchased a $2K gift certificate, so when you add in the tax, it brings the total to nearly the exact amount I have lost today. The salesperson asks what name to put on the certificate and, for a moment, I think he might actually be purchasing it for me. Instead, she slips the certificate into one of the silky pockets of the buttery loaf, and in thirty minutes we've spent $8,000. That's $266 a minute.

As we start to exit, he turns to me and says, "Thanks, this was great."

"It was really fun," I sing, still high from having spent so much money, even if it wasn't mine.

We say our good-byes and head off to our separate cars. I didn't get a present, but I am happy because I have triumphed. I have not asked for anything. I have gone shopping with someone who is loaded and I can handle it. It seems like a badge of honor, but as I pull into my driveway of our home it occurs to me that my entire house could fit inside my friend's master bedroom and that I will either need to paint the exterior or make sure that the sun has set if he ever comes to our place.

In the best of circumstances, our house, with its mixed-matched couches and floor-to-ceiling bookcases, has been generously described by visitors as having the furnishings of English professors. Ones without tenure. In the light of day, our living room couch looks depressed. Literally. That sofa has seen a lot of ass. Jeff purchased this couch before we started dating, so that's seventeen years ago now. He likes to fall asleep watching sports on said sofa. My friend cannot come to our house and sit his oft-photographed posterior on our sagging cushions. My friend cannot use one of our one-and-three-quarters bathrooms. Our downstairs bathroom is tiny and with his big head (most actors have large domed heads), he will think it even smaller. He can't possibly go into that wee room. I will need to expand that loo before he comes over. Retile at least. I don't want him to feel sorry for me.

On the other hand, I would like to ask him to pay for my son's college and my face-lift. During our spree, I mentioned I was thinking about getting one, and he said he didn't think I needed it, which is flattering, but at the same time, I wonder, would he offer if he thought I did?

Would he let me live in his guesthouse if I got divorced? Why did I ever break up with him? Was our somnambulant sex really that much worse than some of the sex I've had when I've been very much awake? It was. Still, what if I threw myself at him and got pregnant? I'd probably only have to fuck him once and I'd be set for the next eighteen years. And better the devil you know wants to fuck you from behind while you pretend to be his mute housekeeper than the devil you don't know. But getting knocked up and entrapping a man is now physically impossible for me. Not that this is something I ever even remotely entertained, but the idea that I can't do it is upsetting. Of course, I am twenty years older and a different race from the woman he married. On top of that, if he can't go in my bathroom, how could I think he'd ever enter my vagina? By the time I climb the flight of stairs to my bedroom, I am so exhausted I have to lie down.

I know in my heart that had we stayed together any longer it would have ended disastrously. I also know he's never coming to my house. That is how it is with our rich and famous friends; we go to their homes, but they do not visit our humble abodes.

This is what it means to live "Hollywood adjacent." Hollywood is a place where nepotism runs rampant and people rise to the top

. . . . . .

on sheer will, talent or membership in the Church of Scientology. Having any family member in the business can give you a colossal leg up, but there are also success stories of people who were once living in their cars or emerge completely from outside the show-business world. Usually those involve the extremely gorgeous, like Hilary Swank, or the uniquely gifted, like Melissa McCarthy. Most of the rest of us have done one if not a dozen failed pilots or dreadful movies, which is how it is that I've acted opposite actors like Anne Hathaway, Shia LaBeouf, Uma Thurman and Patrick Stewart in movies and TV shows no one remembers. You might even have remained friendly with some of the elite. You'll email each other, but it's so hard to nail down plans. You will invite them to your parties, but unless you've scheduled around their demanding social calendar, it won't be possible for them to put in an appearance. You'll see them at a party and you'll be laughing and talking politics and they'll say, "I don't know why we don't get together." But you'll know why. You might live on the same block for seven years, during which time you share major holidays and glasses of wine and swim in their pool. When they tell you they're frustrated by their square footage or are considering adding a bridge from the master bedroom to the pool, you'll know as soon as their TV series gets picked up for a fifth season they'll be moving to a more luxurious abode and that when they do you will not hear from them regularly, if ever again. You will not vacation together. Your kids will go to different schools, and you will find yourself stuck in traffic wondering if you will spend your golden years in a dusty apartment with no air-conditioning and a view of the parking lot in an industrial suburb of Los Angeles known

. . . . . .

for its preponderance of meth labs. You'll look up at a billboard looming over the roadside and see a familiar face staring down at you. You will find it hard to believe that you and they ever breathed the same air, shared confidences, laughed so hard at a lunch table together that cola came out of your noses or that you can be found in clips on YouTube in a lip-lock with that very same person.

Sitting in traffic on my own block a few days later, I receive a text: "Thx, she loved the purse. My mom's birthday is coming up, what should we get her?"

A few weeks later, my husband and I have accepted an invitation for cocktails and dessert at the home of someone my husband worked with years ago. So eager was I to sample the hostess's legendary delectables at this industry soiree that we arrived uncharacteristically half an hour early. Peering into the garden, we can clearly see several well-heeled couples seated at a dinner table finishing a meal. It takes only a few minutes to surmise that we are second-tier guests. We wait in the car until we see other members of our caste arriving. I could have turned around and gone home, but I'd already gotten dressed up, she makes the most amazing trifle and Madonna's pilates teacher just pulled in behind us. Definitely Hollywood adjacent.

. . . . . .

MONSTER BALL

> **Dear God,**
>
> **Please let me remain recognizable to my friends.**

"Ladies, may I show you to a table?" the maître d' asks us.

"'Ladies,'" I whisper to my friend Carla. "Well, at least he didn't 'ma'am' us."

We settle into the seating area of an outdoor restaurant, hold our menus at arm's length and simultaneously reach for our reading glasses.

"Should we order fries?" I ask.

"For old times' sake, we have to, don't you think?"

"They only have sweet potato. Let's put a ton of salt on them."

"And a dipping sauce!" Carla giggles with that same piercing high-pitched laugh that first assaulted my ears in Mrs. Kramer's fifth-grade math class.

"Definitely." If I'm going to eat something stupid, I don't like it to be even remotely healthy. Carla looks remarkably the same as when we saw each other last, but times have changed in Miami Beach. This bistro occupies the space that used to be our favorite greasy spoon. She and I haven't seen each other in thirty years, but we're able to pick up right where we left off. It can be like that with girlfriends, especially if you both always felt like oddballs. It's only fitting that we have this reunion over fried food because we grew up sharing plates of deep-fried clams at our local Howard Johnson before cosmopolitan hotels crowded the coastlines of South Florida.

Every trace of your great-aunt Sylvia's Miami Beach is long gone, but through the miracle of the Internet, even the few friends I've lost track of have been found, and that's how Carla and I have been able to rekindle our friendship.

I treasure my old friends. Or, as one of them recently corrected me, "longtime" friends. *Don't say "old," say "longtime friends."*

You need your sisters. Even though your male friends adore you, they evaporate into thin air at the first mention of a hot flash.

Only a few days earlier, I was heading to a job in New Jersey when Michelle, another longtime friend, was on her way to Long Island to visit her father-in-law, who'd had triple bypass surgery, and she needed to talk. The best we could arrange was a meet-up in the cell phone waiting lot at New York's LaGuardia Airport. Amid a sea of limo drivers and what appeared to be mobile escort services, I jumped out of my rental car and into her minivan. Our sons are the same age. She had big news.

"Pubes."

"No!" I screamed. "Did you see them yourself?"

. . . . . .

"No, I heard about it from my husband."

"Oh my God! That's not happening yet at my house."

"Well, Miles has started shaving."

"Just think, we've known each other since before we started shaving our legs, and we will probably start shaving our faces at the same time. So much to look forward to!" But wait, there's more. She'd taken my advice to stock tampons at her house, and one of her son's friends had gotten her period during his birthday pool party.

"What did you do?" Between us we have only boys, so neither of us has prepared for The Talk. "She'd locked herself in the bathroom and didn't want me to call her mother, so I planted myself outside the door and I just kept repeating, 'So you probably know the way things work down there,' like I was talking about NAFTA. It got very quiet. It only took about twenty minutes, but I was so exhausted afterward I slept for sixteen hours."

"I am not ready for that. You know, it would just be so much easier if we lived together." When my son was a toddler, the idea of built-in babysitters made that FLDS sister-wife concept seem almost palatable. At this age, if it weren't for those starched rayon-blend prairie dresses and the nauseating prospect of having sex with a relative of Warren Jeffs, living in the company of women would once again hold appeal for me.

"Sonya stays with us a lot, doesn't she, Mom?" It's true. She's one of several friends who're time-sharing the divorce couch in our guest bedroom. She's going through a messy separation and stays with us when she's in town for court appearances. The situation could be reversed in the future.

. . . . . .

If I have achieved nothing else, I feel a sense of accomplishment that I've got a (tiny) guest room with a sleeper sofa always available for my girlfriends to visit. I put out fresh towels, roses from the garden and at least one good pillow.*

Many of my friends are turning fifty within months of each other, but we appear to be aging at such variable rates it's almost enough to convince you that the gravitational pull affects people differently. Some of it is genetics at work, and some of it is *work* at work.

"Carla, have you done something? Because you look better now than you did in high school."

"Here's the thing, I always looked thirty years older than I was. My age is just catching up to my face."

"Well, it's not fair," I say between bites. "Jeanette is so stunning now. I think she's had a face-lift and maybe her brow lifted? I'm not really sure what she did. Our friendship was always based on my thinking I was better looking than her, not that she knew that, of course, but now she looks younger than me."

"But does she look younger, or does she just look different from how she used to?" Carla says.

She poses a good question. Cosmetic surgery doesn't really make you look younger, particularly next to someone who is genuinely younger than you. You just look like someone who has had something done. There's also good and bad work, and like porn, you know it when you see it.

---

*I can only hope that my new insistence on always having flowers in our home is adding to the warmth of our place and not making it resemble an assisted-living facility.

. . . . . .

"Well, she doesn't have 'monster face,'" I say. That's a term I use for crossing that line where you no longer resemble your fellow humans. It's a slippery slope. Are nose jobs okay, but a face-lift unacceptable? Lasers good, knives bad? Too much Botox and your face becomes a shiny monolith. Too much filler and you've got Pillow Face. Too much plastic surgery and you look like a Picasso.

I *think* what I want is to age gracefully, to be the best version of myself. But when did I look most like "me"? Was it the "me" I was at forty, or the "me" at twenty?

I felt disappointed and then strangely liberated when in 2011 Gloria Steinem owned up to having had cosmetic procedures done. Steinem said she regretted it, although women having work done and later claiming to regret it seems part of the ritual of getting it done. One might even argue that the quest to look younger is the modern expression of the search for the fountain of youth, which first appears in written records somewhere around 425 BC. Being young and looking youthful are two different things but to appear young is the next best thing, and there are a myriad of choices available for first-worlders.*

None of this pursuit holds any appeal for Carla, having aged into her face. She's had a long and successful career as an FBI profiler and she believes her face gives her added authority in the courtroom.

"Are you in touch with Allison?" I ask.

---

*And it's even cheaper if you can afford to travel to have work done in the third world.

. . . . . .

"No, would I still recognize her?"

"Maybe not. She wears less makeup now than she did in high school. For the last eighteen years she's worked at an animal sanctuary caring for rescued baboons. A few months ago I asked her how she felt about aging and she told me, 'I don't look in the mirror very often. I see myself reflected in the eyes of the primates I'm helping to end their lives with dignity.'"

"I respect that." Carla nods.

"Me too. It's very Jane Goodall—she's one of my heroes. I've always wondered what kind of sunscreen she uses because her skin looks great.* Anyway, Allison is also a regional distributor of Nu Skin antiaging products and offered to sell me a galvanic microdermabrasion facial wand for three hundred and fifty dollars last year."

Nothing makes any sense. In fact, the majority of people who have cosmetic procedures are middle-income earners.† The "soccer-momization" of cosmetic procedures might be the most telling sign that we're in the grip of a collective facial dysmorphic disorder.

When I'm sure that no one in my family is awake, I can be found intently studying websites devoted to disparaging the disastrous things celebrities are doing to their faces, but these

---

*Right after I wrote this, the *New York Times* published the results of the first human study indicating that sunscreen prevents photo-aging. I'm so gratified that something I'm doing should prove useful.

†According to those noted humanitarians, the American Society of Plastic Surgeons, who lobbied and successfully killed what became known as the Bo-tax, a failed effort to balance the U.S. budget on the faces of American women, over half of the American women who seek plastic surgery earn between $30,000 and $90,000 a year.

. . . . . .

are only rivaled by the number of sites decrying the haggard appearance of those who resist going under the knife. Oh, if only these famous women had had the good sense to take Deborah Harry's words to heart, to die young and stay pretty! Debbie Harry, it's worth noting, finding herself still very much alive and kicking, has been extremely forthcoming about having had a cornucopia of improvements. In yet another frightening sign of aging, I don't actually know who most of the Kristens, Kendras and Kates (not the Middleton Kate) are, but sadly I could give a general accounting of their current weight and marital status. Meanwhile, it is doubtful we will see the visages of genuinely fascinating public figures like Jóhanna Sigurðardóttir, former prime minister of Iceland and the first openly gay head of state, Margaret Atwood, Aung San Suu Kyi, and Sonia Sotomayor splashed across tabloid covers—tabloids that I would never, ever consider purchasing but am forced to peruse when I've accidentally on purpose found myself in the longest line at the supermarket.

One of the unexpected consequences of the rise of social media sites is that everyone feels to a certain extent like they are in the public eye, or at least in contact with people they went to high school with and, of course, their exes. If that's not compelling enough, boomers are trying to maintain a youthful appearance in a job market that favors younger employees.

In *About Face*, an HBO documentary with supermodels discussing the loss of beauty, former model Paulina Porizkova claims it is worse for a great beauty to suffer the loss of her youth to the aging process than for us mere mortals. I would like to state for

. . . .

the record that I think that's a load of crap. It's just as big a deal for the rest of us who were never paid $10K to get out of bed. Maybe bigger. Just because you're short doesn't make falling and breaking your hip hurt any less.*

Growing up, I never liked my face. I was born in the 1960s, but I had a face that suggested I was about to be marched across Russian potato fields on a pogrom in the 1890s. I came by this naturally, as a second-generation American with Russian Ashkenazi Jewish roots on both sides of my family.

My face took a ribbing in Miami Beach, where I grew up surrounded by girls with tan, heart-shaped faces, while I was pale, with a long, sad face, and oversized features. Kids called me "nigger lips," which was the worst thing they could think of to call a white girl in the seventies. During a consultation about removing my wisdom teeth, our local oral surgeon took it upon himself to measure my bottom lip and informed my parents it was several centimeters larger than the average Caucasian-American lip. He offered to "normalize" my lips for no extra charge. I might have even been in favor of this idea, but luckily my folks had the sense to dismiss it offhand. At forty-nine my lips have shrunk to an average size, and if I'd had that reduction I would be completely lipless today.

I tried to make my face fit in. I would lie in the sun, slathered in baby oil, cradling a reflecting foil made just for that purpose. When the infamous Farrah Fawcett swimsuit poster came along,

---

*That is something I imagine to be true, but I hopefully won't be able to personally confirm for at least another thirty years.

I got her hairstyle and I could just about manage to make it work, though in pictures, I can see that the Florida humidity prevented my hair from really feathering properly; it just winged. Those frizzy wings, coupled with ten extra high school pounds and the deep tan, made me look like a chipmunk. Luckily, soon after that the Ramones played at a small venue in Fort Lauderdale. It was life-changing. I immediately stopped going out in the sun, adopted thrift shop clothing, dyed my hair a series of artificial colors and never tried to fit in again.

It wasn't until I hit forty that I started to look at my face critically. I became obsessed with the bags under my eyes. They were all I could see when I looked in the mirror. I began to see the bags as something separate from my face, something that needed to be removed. I convinced myself it was a genetic problem. And it is. I am genetically predisposed to look as tired as I actually am.

It took only forty minutes to take out the bags I had spent forty years accumulating. While I was recovering and feeling like a character in Jacqueline Susann's *Valley of the Dolls*, I wrestled with a case of buyer's remorse. Had I tampered with an essential part of myself? I reasoned that we carry eggs from other women, take antidepressants and adopt radical dietary regimens, therapies and lifestyles, so was this luggage under my eyes really indispensable to a definition of myself? What about a mole that became cancerous? Wouldn't I immediately have that removed and never think twice about it? Once my eyes healed I didn't have to worry anymore because it turned out that I had fixed one problem but created another. Now I have too much hollow space under my eyes.

. . . . . .

Even so, I am not immune to the siren song of the latest in-novations to hit the market. I've had things injected in my face that I wouldn't clean my house with. Once or twice a year, I raid my savings to get my fix from a doctor in Beverly Hills who has clearly sized me up as the sucker that I am. I'm not actually sure what he charges, as it seems to vary widely from visit to visit and I suspect his fees have something to do with his mood and his current credit card balance.* I prefer going to someone I don't like. Having been a client of several practitioners of these dark arts, I have learned that none of them are immune to making mistakes and it's just less disappointing if I don't like them in the first place.

I've filled, frozen and ultrasounded, all in the name of what is often referred to as "maintenance." The last time I went to see the wizard, he did an uneven job, and to correct it he added so much Botox over one eyebrow that I could barely open that lid for a month. On one occasion he said, "I have some extra filler. Let me put it in your chin—you need a bigger chin, like mine," and before I could say, *I don't want more chin. I don't like your chin!* he had done it. I hated that extra chinnage, which did fade with time, but still. I used to wonder who would let someone experiment on their face and now I know—me.

"Maintenance" is truly a misnomer because what no one tells you is that it's a zero-sum game. You look the very best immedi-

---

*I worked the door at exclusive nightclubs, and besides the cash salary, I walked away with an ability to recognize good shoes. I was taught that this was a reliable and quick way to assess our clientele. I'd say this doctor enjoys bespoke shoes from London and I've footed the bill.

ately after one of these treatments, while your face is slightly swollen. The swelling restores your face's lost volume in a way that looks more natural than anything you can get on the market today. Once that goes away, the results, if noticeable at all, begin to fade, day by day, until very shortly afterward, sometimes weeks, you look exactly the same as you did the day you forked over an amount that an entire family in Turkmenistan could live on for a year. The similarity of "radio-frequency" nonsurgical face-lifts to electroshock therapy is not something anyone tells you either. Sadly, unlike with ECT, there is no short-term memory loss. I have only myself to blame when recalling the excruciatingly painful jolts of electricity I have paid to have pumped into my face. Studies show that when people believe they are drinking expensive wine, they enjoy it more than when they sample the exact same beverage they're told sells at a lower price point. Perhaps after shelling out so much money, we have to convince ourselves that we've improved our looks. Heroin addicts call it chasing the dragon when you're trying to recapture that first amazing high, and this is much the same fruitless pursuit.*

After the big earthquake eventually hits Los Angeles, it's not hard to imagine desperate women, unrecognizable even to their own personal assistants, roaming the streets of Beverly Hills trying to score black-market Botox. If I were truly enterprising, I would start stockpiling vials of injectables and store them in my

---

*A recent survey indicated that people who've had plastic surgery appeared to have shed only three years on average off of their age. Which three years, I wonder? Fourteen to seventeen were relatively breezy but I barely slept for the first three years of my son's life and if I could reverse that damage, it might be worth it.

AARP refrigerated tote so I could sell them out of the trunk of my car at massively inflated prices. In fact, given the volatility of the stock market, this might be my best hope at funding my retirement.

My grandmothers never grappled with such nonsense. These matriarchs were peasant stock who survived the Depression and had managed to rise to the middle class by the 1950s, and all that effort showed on their faces. They embraced their roles as grandmothers when not only being a grandma but looking like a grandma was a sign of respect. My grandmother Frances always kept a tub of cool, creamy, cucumbery Pond's in her bathroom cabinet. That was as much vanity as she had time and money to afford. She really did have the softest, most glowing skin until her death at eighty-nine, so maybe it worked.

At seventy-five, my mother feels bad about her neck. She's had the benefit and curse of rising just enough into a social strata in which she has longtime friends who can afford to pony up for procedures, while she cannot. My mother, who had the temerity to turn fifty in 1985, the year the United Nations proclaimed International Youth Year, confided that she felt old next to her friends who'd had work done. At the time, I dismissed this as ridiculous, but now I understand the sentiment. Why wouldn't my mother want to age as gracefully as her peers, as the saying goes? It's not a stretch to say that you can get a pretty good idea of someone's economic status at fifty or older by looking at their skin.

"Do you think you'll ever be tempted?" I ask Carla as we finish the very last sweet potato fry.

. . . . . .

"We almost lost my sister-in-law when she went in for a tummy tuck. She had a heart attack on the table. I couldn't put my family through that. I can't ever remember to get any products, either, so everyone is just going to have to live with my face."

"So what exactly do you do as an FBI forensic profiler?"

"It's like putting the pieces of a puzzle together. My specialty is examining audio and visual evidence."

"Well, if I do have any more work done, at least I can hope that you will always recognize me."

"It all depends on how good it is," Carla reminds me as we kiss good-bye.

Here's what I know. I liked my face best in my forties, but I'd like it to stop aging now. My face has progressed past the point where I recognize it as "me." Age can stamp a certain sameness on the face just like plastic surgery. I can't yet wrap my brain around or afford a face-lift, and that's where humility and a sense of humor come in. "Hello, new old face," I say to myself while I brush my teeth in the morning. "Soon you will be gone and I will get to say hello to my next, newer, older face, if I'm lucky."

I love my pals who are going face commando. I respect my friends who are content with their newly renovated faces and I empathize with my peers who want to look, if not younger, then like the best versions of themselves, whatever that may be. I'd just rather not be photographed next to Rhonda, Jannelle, Maureen, Paula or Cynthia. And definitely not Jeanette.

. . . . . .

AREA FIFTY-ONE

> **Dear God,**
>
> **If reincarnation really exists I'd like to be a few inches taller in my next life. And I don't mean hair height.**

"Golden hour," that's what it's called in the film business. The perfect time to shoot a scene outdoors in Los Angeles. The light is soft and flattering, even for women who are certain of their age, and the scorching desert sun doesn't beat down like a police interrogation lamp. It's also an ideal hour to play tennis in the stagnant, heavy heat of late August. That's what my husband, son and I were doing one Sunday night: squeezing in those last minutes of daylight on the Vermont Canyon free tennis courts a few blocks from our home. We'd just about exhausted ourselves when my son looked up in the sky and noticed a V-shaped pattern of lights. Even I had to admit that it looked like a formation, and it did seem to be moving. Fast. Really fast.

"Mom, it's alien spacecrafts."

"No, honey, it's weather balloons or satellites. You know, there are so many military installations here in California, we have no idea what they're doing."

"No, Mom, the lights are so far away, past the stratosphere. It's got to be UFOs. Are you denying that the government has documented real sightings?"

"Sweetheart, that's not true."

"How do you know?"

"Because no one in our government can keep a secret," I said, referring not only to Watergate and Troopergate, but how everyone knows that Eliot Spitzer keeps his socks on during sex.

"What about that secret military base, Area 51?"

"Area 51," I said, "is not that mysterious. It has never been shown to be anything other than an ordinary Air Force base." But I can feel my pulse racing as I peer into the heavens. The tennis courts do kind of look like a landing strip. Are we about to experience a close encounter of the third kind?*

"Would you want to go, Ezra?" I asked. "If aliens landed and invited you onto their ship, would you go with them?"

"Of course, Mom!"

Of course he would. What thirteen-year-old wouldn't want to hitch a ride to the stars?

"Brush your teeth, try to get at least eight hours of sleep a night, and text us pictures—we'll keep you on our phone plan."

---

*In UFO lingo, a close encounter of the first kind is seeing the UFO, the second kind involves some sort of interaction, the third kind is getting on the ship/pod mode of transport. It's beam-me-up-Scotty territory.

The three of us stood there. We peered into the sky. We were the only ones left in the canyon. It was so quiet.

That's when reality set in. There's no chance that I'm going anywhere. I'm too old to be a candidate for interplanetary travel. What would extraterrestrials want with me? To see the effect of the speed of light on the aging body? I'd never make it out of our solar system much less the Milky Way. Besides, if you'd traveled across the universe, wouldn't your first stop on our little blue marble be the White House, The Hague or the Kremlin? How about the South of France for a restorative infusion of Chateauneuf-du-Pape? But there was a time in my life when I was sure they were coming for me.

I've wanted many things in my life, including balancing my checkbook to within even one hundred dollars and summoning the resolve to resist movie theater popcorn, but more than anything I wanted to leave the planet, and I was confident I would get that opportunity. That's what we all believed in the cult I belonged to in the eighties in New York.

Not that it seems any less implausible or makes sense in any way, but many, many people in the eighties belonged to some kind of self-help—or self-hurt—group. Downtown New York was bursting with drugs, transvestites and cheap places for artists to squat or rent. Add to the mix new-age mystics, Buddhist-inspired sects and self-realization fellowships that denied bathroom privileges, and half of the population of lower Manhattan fit into one or more of these categories. The group I was a part of existed because of the abundance of all of those elements, but unlike Werner Erhard's EST seminars, there was no fee, no recruitment, no

. . . .

Scientology secrecy, and you could go to the bathroom anytime you wanted. There was also no unflattering dress code. I was horrified to read in 1997 about the mass suicide of thirty-nine members of the Hale-Bopp UFO sect, who favored boxy jumpsuits and adopted boring monosyllabic unisex monikers. It was also unfathomable to me that anyone would have been content to live with sect leaders "Do" and "Ti" on a 3.4-acre property with a pool and tennis courts but be housed in dormitory-style rooms with bunk beds. Ridiculous! But snagging a seat on a spaceship? I was on board with that idea.

How I ended up in a UFO cult is directly related to my moving to New York in the fall of 1980. I had fair to middling SAT scores and a grade point average good enough to make me a decent candidate for NYU acceptance, but I had other advantages working in my favor: desperation and good timing. I remain convinced I was accepted because I cried and begged to be admitted during my interview. I hear this doesn't work anymore in the college application process, but as luck would have it, I had specifically requested placement in their Experimental Theatre Wing, a fledgling program that was actively soliciting students for enrollment.* The night before my audition I had attended a student production. There was no set, no lighting to speak of, no costumes and no script. The cast members, a man and a woman, both of them androgynous-looking, were attired solely in black, as was everyone in attendance. Halfway through the performance, the

---

*I had the opportunity to interview an admissions officer on NPR about current standards at NYU. She assured me that with my grades, scores, and crying I would have absolutely no chance whatsoever of being admitted to the school today.

. . . . . .

woman mounted the piano, sang a self-composed song of disaf-fection and began screeching, "I'm fucking a piano," at which point a real pizza delivery guy distributed pies to both the cast and the audience. I had no idea what it meant, but I knew that the performers wanted to change the perception of language, pizza and maybe the world. I had to become a part of this eccentric and iconoclastic community.*

I wasn't merely heading off to college; I was hoping to find a new family. Such is the promise that the theatrical community holds. Whenever a friend lets me know that their kid has been bitten by the drama bug, my reaction is always the same: "Call me immediately! What is going wrong over at your house? We've got to nip this in the bud!"

It's possible I was just hardwired to be the kind of person who looks at other families and longs to be part of them, who thinks that everyone else's life looks better than my own, but it's also possible that childhood experiences carved deep grooves in my brain, making a certain path irresistible for me.

Growing up, my family weathered numerous dramatic rever-sals of fortune that to a child seemed to happen overnight, like magic.

Sometimes we'd be eating fried chicken off the mahogany pull-down trays in the back of my father's Rolls-Royce, and sometimes it was Kentucky Fried right out of the bucket. Dad's love of cars proved a reliable barometer for our bank account.

---

*That performer, the multitalented Gayle Tufts, is now a prominent chanteuse in Germany.

. . . . . .

Good times meant matching Mercedeses for my folks, but I might come home and see a Chevrolet in the driveway where a Jaguar had been parked a few weeks prior. I still dream of that Jaguar. The compact XJ6 in the 1970s was the Petit Trianon of luxury cars, with its leather interior, polished wood and chrome fixtures. It also never worked. We took turns sitting in it, basking in its elegance, as it sat in our driveway, the salty Floridian air eating away at its undercarriage.

This lifestyle had its advantages. There were vacations in the Bahamas and Cozumel, regular exposure to classical music, art, and plays by Noel Coward. There were also unique educational opportunities. I was the only student at my school who could spot an FBI plainclothes agent. In 1978, my parents were invited to a party on the yacht of an Arab sheikh who claimed to be looking to invest in American business ventures. What they didn't know was that they, along with other business types who worked at the margins, were being used as shills in an FBI investigation that became known as Abscam, intended to ferret out dirty politicians. My mother maintains that she knew something was wrong because the appetizers served included Ritz crackers topped with Cheez Whiz. Later, the Justice Department would accuse the FBI of entrapment, and months of investigations of all the parties involved ensued. I learned to spot the flat paint on their bland American sedans before answering the door to poker-faced agents wearing ill-fitting polyester suits and reflective sunglasses. I was instructed to tell anyone that came to our door that my folks weren't at home. Ever. They were never at home. I also became well versed in avoiding creditors' phone calls. One night as my father and I were watching *Star Trek* reruns, I said, "Who on earth would have their house mortgaged to Phil Rizzuto and The Money Store?!" We did. That's who. My family was way ahead of the curve: we were carrying two or three mortgages long before everyone in the country was underwater. It was both exciting and terrible, the perfect combination that leads one to pursue a life in show business or to fall under the spell of a guru. Or both.

All of these experiences left me longing for what appeared to be a stable home. I'd attach myself to friends whose parents had jobs I could understand, like architect, dentist or accountant. I pined to be adopted by them or by any of my teachers who showed an interest in me, and during that thirty-minute performance and a three-day stay in the city, I fell into a love affair with New York that I've never gotten over. New Yorkers seemed like one big extended family to me.*

But I found something even better than the theatrical community. A family who professed love for me not only in this life but in past lives as well. This was a bond way stronger than plain old Jewish guilt. It was destiny.

How do you meet someone who claims to channel disembodied spirits? It happened the way so many things do, especially when you're young: through someone you're sleeping with. That my college curriculum included learning to whirl like a dervish made the idea of someone entering transcendental states seem

---

*My immediate goal became to get listed in the New York phone book. I thought you had to do something really great to get in there.

perfectly reasonable. It was sometime in that first year in New York when my boyfriend became acquainted with new-age seekers and he introduced me to this group.

Van Zandt hailed from Texas and had a bigger-than-life personality. He was only thirty-five when we met, but as I was nineteen and in college, he seemed decades older. He was an accomplished classical pianist who preferred idiosyncratic composers like Scriabin but supported himself as a church organist in the outer boroughs of New York City. I rather doubt he ever mentioned his paranormal activities at his church gigs. A gay man who established himself in the post–Stonewall liberation West Village of Manhattan, he made annual treks to China, Tibet and other parts east to add to his collection of antique textiles, and frequented the club scenes. He didn't wear a turban on his head or tell fortunes by staring into a crystal ball, though he did have both, but he did, every Friday night for the better part of seven years, give psychic readings and channel spirits in his incense-filled living room.

Van Zandt charged no money, nor profited in any way other than being a much-sought-after dinner guest. There were always hangers-on requesting psychic predictions, but he was such a handsome, charismatic and warm person, he probably would have been just as popular without the readings.

I was instantly absorbed into the fold. We were told by the entity he channeled that we had all been part of a family in ancient Egypt. And not just any family but a rather prominent one. The personage, David, whom Van Zandt channeled, informed us that he was the reincarnation of the pharaoh Akhenaten, often cred-

. . . . . .

ited as the father of monotheism. The others in our group were sisters, aunts, uncles and priests of the high court. I was one of his cherished daughters, Meritaten. Akhenaten was a much more interesting pharaoh, much cooler than the better known Tut, the boy king. Akhe was an avatar that advanced the culture in many ways, including being the first pharaoh to allow depictions of himself in activities of his everyday life, a move toward populism that was so radical for a monarch during this period that historians suspect he was killed for such a heretical action. This was a far more exalted heritage than being the great-granddaughter of a junk dealer who traveled from shtetl to shtetl on a swayback mule. Because of this connection, we threw ourselves into study of this ancient time period. You want to know anything about the eighteenth dynasty, just ask me, I know almost as much as if I had lived then myself. I would often go to the Metropolitan Museum of Art to visit their collection of artifacts, items I believed I had called my own only three thousand years earlier.

Ours was a loose affiliation of artist types. We began to refer to ourselves as Members of the Council. These were self-appointed positions; even though we had lived as nobility in a previous life, we were a very egalitarian body. There was a debonair gentleman who worked as a very successful nose in the perfume industry, a busboy, a buyer for a prestigious fashion house, the girlfriend of a bona fide rock star and there were always colorful gay men, lovers of Van Zandt. They were the exact opposite of the members in the last organization I had belonged to, the Temple Beth Shalom Youth Group.

We were also told of numerous humble incarnations spent in

. . . . . .

abject poverty. This lent some verisimilitude to the narrative. You can't be a princess in every life, right?

We were also in contact—regular contact—with aliens. An ancient alien race was monitoring the earth from electronic devices buried under the poles. This highly evolved species had seeded the planet, and they were coming back for what was going to be the first recorded contact in history. This event was scheduled to occur on an island off the coast of Sardinia on November 21, 1995. We would be returning to our true home, a planet somewhere in a distant galaxy. The specifics of the landing weren't clear, and the subject of our needing to leave our bodies behind was never broached. I believe we all held an image of a giddy Richard Dreyfuss boarding the light-filled craft in Spielberg's *Close Encounters of the Third Kind* in our collective mind's eye.* We were given the coordinates of the star system where this faraway outpost was located. Sadly, I have not retained what one could postulate was some of the most important information ever communicated to humans, outside of Ben Affleck's elegiac testament to the futility of holding grudges in his 2013 Oscar acceptance speech.

I was also told I was going to win an Academy Award. Presumably this would happen before our departure, as it would not only be a tough commute to return from our intergalactic journey for the ceremony, but finding a stylist and having fittings for a dress would be difficult transplanetarily.

I was two years into college when my parents suffered a major

---

*As a parent, when I see that movie, circa 1978, it doesn't make sense that Dreyfuss would leave his kids behind without so much as a good-bye, but Steven Spielberg's first child wasn't born until 1985, which might explain that story point.

......

financial setback and I dropped out of school. I had just returned from a semester abroad when I got the news. I went from studying art and architecture in London to punching a time clock and handing out flyers on the street for Arby's dressed as a clown. Actually, the clown getup turned out to be a total bonus as I was working in my own neighborhood and was grateful for the anonymity the makeup afforded. Alone and on my own in the city, this confluence of events caused me to rely even more on my new family for emotional support.*

Why Van Zandt felt such a great affection for me is a mystery I will never solve. He had absolutely nothing to gain from me, but his love was unconditional and unbounded. Outside of his role as a medium, Van Zandt was very down-to-earth. The kind of guy who reveled in a great find at a thrift store, loved his cheeseburger and fries after our sessions and enjoyed amyl nitrite and anal sex, though we never got into deep discussions about either of the latter. He was quite simply the best gay dad a girl could ever hope for.

I never asked critical questions, like why our artsy band was chosen to usher in the new age and not the legions of religious adherents who have dedicated their entire lives to achieving enlightenment. On the face of it, there wasn't much to recommend me, in particular, as a representative of our planet. I didn't have any scientific knowledge that could be useful on a long journey across the universe. In fact, I had enrolled in an astronomy

------

*Nobody wanted those flyers. I would throw them in the trash and sit out the rest of my shift in an alley, crying and working my way through my dog-eared copy of *Tess of the D'Urbervilles.*

. . . . . .

class at NYU so I could gain more understanding of my future voyage but never made it to more than a handful of the classes. The seminars had a narcoleptic effect on me—these were the dark ages before really good coffee could be found on every corner of the city, and I attended these lectures on nothing more potent than watery coffee-shop drip. Neither was I particularly athletic, an attribute that might indicate my physical readiness to undertake an intergalactic jaunt, but I didn't spend a great deal of time questioning the improbability of it all. After all, I was the reincarnation of the daughter of Akhenaten. Favorite daughter, I might add.

And yet I had no problem deeming other mediums I encountered as inauthentic. On one occasion, a few of us trekked to Brooklyn to see a woman channel tree fairies for a fee of twenty-five dollars per head. "What a total phony," I remember saying on our way out. "*Tree fairies*, have you ever heard of anything so silly?"

I neglected to discuss this part of my life with professional colleagues even though my confidence and fragile self-esteem were dependent on the assurances of success that I'd received from this adoptive father mostly while he was in a trance.

It was at this time that AIDS was beginning to cut a swath across the gay community. Several men in our group died swiftly, as was common in the early years. Then Van Zandt was diagnosed. The members of our group rallied and we took turns spending the night with him, placing cold compresses on his forehead, helping him to perform the basic functions of life. As the youngest in our group, I was only asked to carry out a small share of the

. . . . . .

caretaking; all the while, Van Zandt kept urging me to move to California. I didn't want to leave him, but he simply wouldn't take no for an answer. He was already in the last months of his life, encamped at Saint Vincent's Hospital, when I packed up my bags and left New York. I landed in Los Angeles the same day an industry-wide strike was called, but I'd already given up my apartment so there was no turning back. I got a job hostessing at a nightclub frequented by Russian mobsters who tipped me in cocaine and black-market blue jeans, but I stuck it out and kept tabs on Van Zandt. A few months later, while on location with the first acting job I'd booked in California, an unmemorable movie of the week titled *Where the Hell's That Gold?!!?* with Willie Nelson in Alamosa, Colorado, I learned of his passing.*

His death was devastating for me. The group disbanded and I lost contact with everyone. I didn't actually know many of them as anything but the affectionate nicknames Van Zandt had given them: Rabbit, Angel, Feather or Miss Thing.

When the aliens didn't arrive on the appointed date, I reasoned it could have been a scheduling error. You're traveling across the universe back to the world you seeded, but you have to stop to refuel or seed a civilization on another planet, or maybe their concept of time is simply different from ours. So what if they were running a few hundred or even several thousand years late—what's the difference in the bigger scheme of things? Maybe those computers buried under the poles needed to be recali-

---

*The question and exclamation marks are not my commentary; they are, sadly, part of the title.

brated. My cell phone needs to be reset for time zones, and those babies were placed under the ice millions of years ago and were sorely in need of tech support. They had to have a supremely advanced society, but wasn't it possible their economy had tightened and that the 1995 scheduled voyage to planet earth had been put on the back burner in the same way NASA projects get redlined? To date, the Academy Award prediction has not come to pass, either, at least not in this or any currently known dimension.

It was around that time that I had one of my first celebrity sightings in Los Angeles, the actress Rebecca De Mornay reading *CoDependent No More* at the Sunset Car Wash. I took that as a sign, the last sign I would ever look for, to put down my wand and take up a hammer. I worked on my craft and religiously avoided anything that smacked of magical thinking or mysticism. Except for patchouli and sandalwood incense. I still love the smell of a séance.

By the time I started my own family, my relationship with nonmagical realism was firmly established. If you've ever tried to find a preschool in an urban area, you know that it's more all consuming than fulfilling a destiny, even one that spans thousands of years. But this period in my life is an endless source of churning remorse at four a.m., when the middle-of-the-night hormone dip jolts me awake. It's at the top of an inventory I call Regrets: The Short List.

Time Spent with People in Trances
If I was looking for a new family, why didn't I just join a sorority? Why didn't I take classes in directing instead of spending

time trying to have an out-of-body experience? I should have learned how to play more than the three chords I know on the guitar instead of comparing my facial features to those of three-thousand-year-old stone carvings. I should have worked as a stripper. Having worked in the sex trade would be less embarrassing than having spent seven years of my life communing with the spirit world. Thank goodness Instagram wasn't around, or I'd be spending the next few lifetimes deleting photographs in which I am costumed as the princess Meritaten. If only I had befriended a psychic who'd seen a medical degree in my future, I'd have a much larger 401(k) today.

The Ones That Got Away

Real estate is a most seductive regret. I've worn deep grooves in my brain mulling over lost opportunities. The $800-a-month loft in Tribeca that was over two thousand square feet, which shared a kitchen wall with Robert De Niro's place, I recently saw listed for $15 million. There was that spacious two-bedroom with floor-to-ceiling windows in Chelsea—$70,000 in 1984. I didn't have enough money to even be looking at places to buy, but I should have found it somehow, even if it meant calling Phil Rizzuto. It would be worth over a million today. That midcentury house my husband and I didn't buy on top of a hill, where you can't hear freeway traffic. It had one more bathroom, was priced less than ours and would be worth over a million today. The words "worth a million today" replay over and over, until I move on to the next set of regrets.

. . . . . .

The Ones That Didn't Get Away

Why did I feel so compelled to date Giancarlo, John Travolta's feet, and David Renaldi? Giancarlo was probably a lovely person, but sadly, my Italian is so limited, I never understood a word he said. "I was John Travolta's feet stand-in in *Saturday Night Fever*," was a line that successfully got my pants off in my twenties. To his credit, Gary claimed ownership of the infamous strutting feet in the electrifying opening sequence of that film. David Renaldi was a starving artist who lived in a tenement building with a bathtub in the kitchen and no bathroom. There was a water closet in the hallway, a tiny room with carpeting and a rotting door that didn't close entirely. It had no lock and was shared with the tenants from several apartments. I developed a urinary tract infection from those long waits. Then again, through a recent Google search, I've learned Mr. Renaldi appears to have a thriving law practice focused on constitutional law, something I find endlessly fascinating, so maybe the regret is why didn't I date him longer. I imagine he's got unfettered access to modern plumbing. One-night-stand guy whose last name I never knew and first name I can't remember but who'd recently been discharged from the Navy, where he'd discovered he was bisexual—let's add him to the list, too.

The Lost Tears

I spent the winter of 1992 weeping over the loss of my bedroom drapes to my ex-husband. It wasn't worth it; window treatments can be replaced, but I can never get back three months in my early thirties.

. . . .

I See You Made an Effort

It occurred to me one morning at four a.m. that everyone else might have been a part of Van Zandt's group for shits and giggles, as the saying goes, except me. I hung on every word, rarely dating anyone, moving to a new apartment or making a business decision without consulting him first. Everyone else was just living in the eighties. I might have been the only one actually in a cult.

Then again, maybe not.

Almost twenty years after his death, an email arrived with Van Zandt's name in the subject line. I recognized the name of the sender immediately as someone from our group, even though I hadn't thought of her in almost as many years. Let's call her Q. The email was addressed to Members of the Council. Q was writing to let us know that she had devoted much of the last twenty years combining over one hundred and thirteen cassette tapes, and four reel-to-reel recordings into CD compilations of our sessions. Maybe I wasn't the only one in the cult. She had inserted his name into her surname. Possibly legally? She wanted to know if we would like to receive copies of the CDs she'd made.

This might be my chance to rewrite the past. My chance at closure or to reconnect. I considered the responses I might compose.

Dear Q,
   Did you ever and do you still believe that we were
fated to travel to other worlds? Why do you suppose the
landing didn't happen?

Or: Where's my Academy Award?

. . . . . .

Or: Do you feel lost without our friend, or are you still in contact with him? Are there messages you've received intended for me?

Or: Have you ever considered availing yourself of talk or drug therapies?

Before I wrote anything, I asked myself what would my most evolved fifty-year-old self do? Then I realized how shortsighted I'd been. I'd been so focused on turning fifty, I hadn't thought about what happens the day after I turn fifty. I'll be *in* my fifties. I'm becoming Area Fifty-One. I'd cultivated an air of mystery, but it turns out I'm far more ordinary than I ever expected and that's okay, even something of a relief. I am my own family. I don't need a celestial lineage or the answers to any of my questions anymore. I can't afford to spend one more minute of my ever-shortening life punishing myself for the choices I made in my twenties, because I will be leaving the planet. I will have a close encounter with Death, who will remove me from the planet swifter than an extraterrestrial airlift. Thank you, fifty.

So what I wrote was this:

Dear Council Member,
I would love to have copies of the CDs. Thank you.

The CD set arrived. I put it in my desk, where I expect it will remain unopened.

. . . . . .

"Mom, I can't see the lights anymore, but I know what I saw." My son's voice snaps me back to reality.

"Okay, let's go home," I say, breathing the longest sigh in my entire forty-nine years.

As we get into the car, I ask my husband if he would have married me if I'd told him I had once believed I was going to leave the planet in the company of friendly alien life-forms. "No," he said without hesitation and a quizzical look. I can't blame him. If he'd ever said anything like that before we'd tied the knot, I'd have insisted that he undergo a psychiatric evaluation and sign a blood oath declaring he had no intention of departing the planet anytime in the foreseeable future.

"We can check the Internet and see if anyone else saw anything," I say as we pull up to our home. But we don't. Once inside, we breeze past the artifacts that decorate the walls of our dining room: a handwoven Tibetan tapestry, two antique wooden Chinese window lattices and a small fragment of an Indian fabric, intricately laced with gold and silver thread. All inherited from my dear friend Van Zandt. We head into the kitchen. We've got dinner to heat up. Dishes to wash, showers to take and our favorite Sunday night TV to watch together. Just an ordinary night on earth with my family.

I'M MEDITATING AS
FAST AS I CAN

> **Dear God,**
>
> **Isn't there some shortcut to slowing down?**

I'm seated at a birthday party next to a woman who is singing the praises of Vedic Meditation. She's in her sixties and is making that decade look effortlessly appealing. She's the heir to a banking fortune, with homes in Nantucket and Los Angeles, so one might reasonably conclude that financial woes are not about to give her frown lines anytime soon, but still, people have been unhappy with more, so hers seems like a compelling endorsement.

She tells me there's a free introductory lecture this very week with her teacher, who has flown in from Australia, so what do I have to lose? I announced my intention to attend somewhere between the salad and the entrée and before the coffee was served

I'd gotten the address, time and date. As it turned out, because I was writing without my reading glasses, I got a few minor details wrong. I arrive at the yoga studio and find I'm an hour early and a day late for the freebie.

"If you're up for it, you can start meditating with us tonight. A beginner's course starts in an hour. It's five hundred dollars and it's a four-day-long commitment. You can come at either nine a.m. or six p.m. for two hours each day," Bradley, the instructor's impossibly good-looking assistant, tells me.

"Sign me up."

I didn't sign up because, as Bradley suggests, "It was meant to be," no, I enrolled in the course because it had taken twenty or thirty texts and emails, and as many phone calls, to coordinate our carpool so I could leave the house on a school night. I was just too embarrassed to go home and face my family, and it was too early in the day to start drinking.

I am not looking to start a meditation practice for fun. No one takes up a rigorous practice of any kind at forty-nine for fun. That would be like suggesting I'd just given up sugar for fun and not because I'd just been diagnosed as prediabetic after a routine blood draw. No, I know I need to start meditating because middle age is turning me into a raving maniac.

It might start like this. A simple meeting with our investment guy. He tells me there's good news and good news, and which do I want first? Either one? My retirement plan is recovering some value. I wasn't wiped out during the recent financial downturn because the majority of the money in my account was in cash.

"I went to cash against your advice, right?"

. . . . . .

"Yes, and now your IRA is worth almost as much as it was back in 2001."

"What's the other good news?"

"I'm moving to a new firm, and that's good news for you, because at the new place, I won't have to recommend their investment products. I can recommend just the ones I think are the best for you."

"So, what you're saying is that for the last ten years you've been recommending things that aren't in my best interest, but now you'll be able to?"

"Yes!"

"This is the best you've got?"* I can almost hear my brain cells exploding.

The churning rage might continue when my husband takes to singing "I am woman, hear me cough" around the house because my nightly glass of red wine is giving me a persistent dry cough that I thought was allergies but my husband has correctly recognized as acid reflux. I am downing Tagamet by the fistful. Caffeine, chocolate and red wine, the anchors of my food pyramid, turn out to make acid reflux worse, making me even angrier. Anger, it turns out, is bad for acid reflux, and that is making me furious.

Giving up sugar makes me positively blow a gasket. It's not like I appear overweight, so to be denied sugar because of the results of blood work seems like a sneaky ploy on behalf of my body to

---

*Two months after that meeting, the papers are filled with the UBS two-billion-dollar trading scandal. This is the new, more transparent firm my guy has switched to.

. . . . . .

remind me that not looking old doesn't have anything to do with being old. Cutting sugar out of my diet, it turns out, does not increase my energy level in any measurable way. I'm down to one good hour a day. An hour I would prefer to enjoy hopped up on a sugar high.

Internet passwords have the power to reduce me to a state of sheer madness. There's just no way I can remember them all. This means I have to change my passwords on a regular basis. However, some of the sites I visit won't accept the same password more than ten times, and if I pick something that isn't a repeat of one I've already used, then I can't remember the new one. Sometimes, I can't remember my user name, so I have to create new email accounts just to access those sites, and if I forget the passwords to those new email addresses, I'll never get back into them, if I can even remember what these new email addresses are in the first place. Recently, I was forced to resort to calling my cell phone provider when I couldn't remember how to access my online account. When the operator asks why I don't know my user name, I give what will no doubt become my new go-to excuse: "I'm fifty." She tells me she can't accept my payment unless I produce the information I entered on their website, something I can't even remember doing in the first place.

"Are you saying that random people call and want to pay phone bills that aren't their own?"

"Yes," she replies, just to piss me off further.

"Really," I say. "How do I get someone to do that? Because that sounds fantastic. Until then, will you please, please, please take my fucking money!"

. . . . . .

I keep trying to remind myself to write down all the sites and the codes, and I can't remember to do that, either. I've also gone paperless with my bank and investment accounts, so if my memory diminishes even further, no one, including me or my family, who has no idea where I even do my banking, will ever gain access to these accounts. This might be the point of all the rules and regulations surrounding gaining access to your own accounts—it might be a vast conspiracy by the banking industry. How many abandoned accounts of mine might already be languishing in cyberspace?

And why? Why? Why, if I am one of your most treasured women friends, are you sending me emails that require me to foist unwanted emails on ten friends within thirty minutes? What kind of invitation demands a response that is divisible by two? Can't we meet up so I can "sit at your table" in person? I'll bring a bottle of rosé or white—no red wine, since you might have reflux as well. Emails that threaten retribution from one deity or another should I break the chain might one day make me go postal.* What kind of God is so micromanaging that he/she/it would count the number of times I forwarded something before granting me any kind of luck or blessing? What if I send said email to ten people but one of the addresses is outdated or it lands in someone's spam folder? Do I still get the good karma I am due for my effort? Is this Internet God the same deity called upon to stop genocides and famine, or is there a subcontractor supreme

---

*Ironically, when the senders of chain mail went to the post office instead of the Internet, far fewer annoying missives were sent; at least it took some effort and the cost of a stamp to send that crap.

. . . . . .

being whose purview is solely cyberspace? Does the same God monitor the innumerable variety of email providers? Lord, that's an expansive kingdom to rule over. I just lost an entire cluster of brain cells on that one.

That's why I'm writing out a check for five hundred dollars that I can't afford. Bradley mentions that the five hundred dollars really doesn't begin to cover our teacher's expenses, and besides, "Maybe you can't afford *not* to take this course," adds Bradley. I mentally add his name to my things-that-make-me-enraged list.

The first thing I learn is that I have neglected to bring the offering of flowers that are traditional in the presence of a Vedic yoga teacher. Luckily, our teacher, Thom, doesn't blanche when I place a few daisies in front of him that I've rescued from the lobby trash can. Five hundred dollars *and* flowers? He's not a cheap date.

He informs us that the practice we are about to learn is an ancient form that TM, Transcendental Meditation, is based on. Uh-oh. TM, don't they advertise yogic flying? Red alert, red alert! Stay away from things that promote levitating. It also seems like yogic flying is like something you'd have to dress for, and I'm in my now-standard everyday wear—a wrap dress—so even flapping could prove embarrassing.

He promises that we'll be able to reverse the aging process. I feel dubious about this claim until he adds that Mick Jagger practices this form of meditation. I only hope Mick Jagger paid more than the five hundred dollars I paid, as I'd hate to be subsidizing our teacher's travel bill to and from Mick's pad in London.

Our teacher tells us that meditating will help us stay in the

......

present moment. The sign of not being in the present, he goes on, is when you find yourself rehearsing the future and reviewing the past. His voice interrupts my strategizing how I will tell my husband that our son's braces aren't covered by our new dental plan and a wave of remorse over a job I turned down more than a decade ago. Teach's got me on that account.

He further explains that when we're not able to access our brain's full capacity our reactions become ingrained and we're no longer innocent to experience. Uh-oh, this is a problem, because it's not my first time at this dance. I've torn through yoga practices like others sample tapas. Is this endeavor destined to become just another one of my failed attempts? But when Thom says this form is purely a practical technique and we don't need any special spirituality, that we need to "just do it," I decide I'll give it a shot. Twenty minutes a day, twice a day. I hunker down.

We close our eyes and I instantly know I'm great at this. I might be the best meditator in the world. Exactly three and one-half minutes have passed.

I close my eyes again, and the remaining seventeen minutes pass quickly. Thom congratulates us on having completed the first meditation of the rest of our lives; only 14,600 minutes of sitting to go this year.

The next day, after a brief distraction about how silly it is to spell "Tom" with an "h," I complete my first sitting and I feel, if not the bliss that Thom promised, an immense amount of joy. I receive a group email asking me to join in an intercessory prayer circle and though the addresses are not even bcc'ed, I lightheartedly chuckle and delete it. After my second meditation that day,

. . . . . .

another email arrives informing me that one of the recipients of that very missive has enlisted her horses into prayer and do any of us realize just how powerful those horses are at helping manifest healing, and the meditation must be working, because I simply hit reply all, with the response "Neigh-be not, but keep it up!"

Mistakes were made. I try meditating in a variety of locales, even in the subways of NYC, until I run into a YouTube video of a rat crawling up the face of a sleeping man on the train.

Our teacher tells us our children will be so happy to see us so relaxed. Not my son.

"Are you going to kill me in my sleep, Mom?"

"No, I'm going to do it while you're awake. Why would you ask me that?"

"It's like you had a psychotic break. You're so weird."

"It's called calm."

"Well, you seem stoned!"

One month into the practice, I become convinced I have been given a bad mantra. Why didn't I get a good one? If I were younger and cuter, Thom would have given me a better mantra. Why is mine so boring? He said there are a number of mantras, and he's chosen the one that is best for each of us, but maybe there is just one and that's why the gurus always insist you keep it a secret.

I keep at it, because with meditation when I am handed a flyer by a person in flip-flops and a T-shirt that reads I SEE DUMB PEOPLE outside a natural-foods store, I say, "Thanks." I look down and see that it says "Hi, I'm David. I'd love to tell you about Herbalife supplements." I politely return it.

"You're missing an opportunity to learn something."

. . . . . .

"I know." I smile and keep walking.

Without meditation, I'd find it irresistible not to answer, *Really? Really, you want to teach me something? You, who are a grown man who leaves the house in flip-flops and derivative T-shirts, want to tell me about becoming an Herbalife dealer? I'm in Bill Ackman's camp, mister!* I'm not going to end up with bottles of pseudo-supplements rotting in my garage and knowingly enlist my friends in a scam just so I can earn a commission. No, thank you, I would rather be filleted than take your flyer!* I still think this, but I don't say it out loud. See why I need to sit every day?

Since then I've meditated while trapped in a car during a blizzard, in planes, in bathrooms, in a photo booth in a mall, and while having dental surgery. Closing my eyes and repeating my dreary mantra turns out to be as reliable an antidote to a Parent-Teacher Association treasurer's report as I've yet to find. As it turns out, I am not the best meditator in the world; in fact, I suck at it. I don't expect to ever get better at it, but I'm doing it anyway. Sucking is one of the unexpected gifts aging has given me. As a younger person I was a perfectionist. I was an inveterate cheater at anything that required patience, like board games, math and monogamy. There's something wonderfully satisfying about acknowledging your mediocrity and still persevering, except in sudoku. I don't understand sudoku. I never have, I never will, I can't even look at it without getting a headache, and the fact that

---

*In February 2012, billionaire hedge-fund managers Bill Ackman and Dan Loeb entered into a billion-dollar wager on whether Herbalife is a pyramid scheme or a multilevel marketing business.

. . . . . .

it's been shown to ward off Alzheimer's fills me with a fury that even meditation can't cure.

Here is the inner monologue of the mediocre meditator:

Pablo Escobar. What ever happened to him, and what's the name of that Latino actor who plays both drug lords and cops?

What time is it?

I can't believe I bought a house that you can hear the freeway from even though it's over a mile away. Damn it. Never buy a house without checking it out at night when the neighborhood is quiet.

Foot falling asleep. Again. What percentage of people meditating have a foot that falls asleep? A lot. A lot percent.

Neck is thrusting forward. Need to work on posture. I've got to hang on to every bit of my five foot four and three-quarters as long as I can. My grandmother Frances shrank to the size of a ladybug.

Buy calcium supplements. With magnesium for better absorption.

I wonder how many students at five hundred dollars a head Teach needs to rope in for him to relax during his meditation?

I love the weight of the cat sleeping on me. I miss my son sleeping on me. Scratching a cat's head has been shown to produce alpha waves. I loved scratching my son's head. I hope I didn't cause his bald spot with my enthusiastic cradle cap-picking.

Why can't I make chicken marsala? I should have a signature dish before I die. Even my mother, who rarely cooked, made a well-regarded beef wellington. If I could make a gluten-free beef wellington, I could open a food truck and corner the market on comfort food that has fallen out of fashion. We will need to serve

. . . . . .

chicken kiev, shrimp scampi and a tuna casserole topped with fried onions from a can. Must perfect recipe before son goes to college, because it's not a signature dish unless you've made it for your kids.

Why did I only have one kid? Who will he be able to laugh about me with when I am gone? Need to do more embarrassing things in front of his friends to create shared memories for him. Try leaving door open when getting out of shower next time one of his friends comes over. No. That is wrong. Very wrong. Very icky. Don't do that. Don't think that. What time is it? Lord, how can twenty minutes pass so slowly?

Muffins are not cake. They're round, and that's totally different.

Very few things stand the test of time. Nothing I do will be remembered when I am dead. My son asked me who Marilyn Monroe was the other day. How many more minutes until I can Google pictures of her before her nose job? People always forget she had work done.

Only scientific inventions, Twinkies and Shakespeare have stood the test of time. I bet that actor whose name I can't remember who plays drug kingpins trained in Shakespeare.

If I had thirty thousand dollars, I could build an extra bathroom.

How tiny are those tiny houses?

If my husband and I each had our own tiny house, we could have our own tiny bathrooms.

I don't know what Susan Sarandon had done, but her neck looks fantastic.

. . . . . .

I hope I don't get a dowager's hump.

If Suze Orman really does retire and goes sailing around the world, how many bathrooms will her boat have, and how tiny will they be?

Zucchini bread isn't cake. It's a loaf and that's totally different.

Whose pink sock is that balled up in the corner and what am I supposed to do with it? My son loses so many socks and kids are always leaving single socks at our house, what am I supposed to do with them? Why can't there be just one sock that everyone wears, like the Mao jacket for feet! The Universal Sock. Yes!

The Universal Sock will come in two colors, white and black. Surely we can all agree that socks don't need to come in any other colors? If we need socks to express our individual flair, then we've got bigger problems, right? Isn't that what beanies are for? And earrings? The sock will come in three fabrics: cashmere, wool and cotton. Sizes: small, medium and large. They will all look exactly the same so if you lose your job and need to down-grade, your old socks will still match any lesser socks you will purchase in the future. Totally egalitarian footwear. This will be a money saver, since you will need to purchase fewer socks as you will no doubt gain socks that are shed by kids and other house-guests. You'll make better use of the socks you have as you fold together stray singletons. As the industry constricts, jobs will disappear, so we'll create work for the unemployed collecting left-over colored socks to make into sweaters for the residents of Portland, clothing for dolls and leggings for cats. In the same way that people who don't use the Internet will eventually die off, leaving a planet populated by humans who never have to wonder

. . . . . .

what people they went to high school with are having for dinner, most will forget there were any other socks and won't miss them at all. Sure, in the distant future, bands of nonconformists determined to exercise their freedom to wear colorful socks will form a liberation movement: Free Our Colored Socks, FOCS, will become a rallying cry for the small population oppressed by the tyranny of dichromatic hosiery, but until then, we will be united and status equalized by our feet.

Miguel Sandoval! He was amazing in that movie about Pablo Escobar, *Blow*. Is it considered memory loss if you can eventually come up with the name you were trying to remember? What time is it?

Okay, it's only been nineteen minutes but who's counting? I'm just going to round up to twenty. Only 13,400-ish minutes of meditation to go this year.

I deserve some cake.

SANDWICHED

> **Dear God,**
>
> **My sandwich is biting into me; isn't it supposed to be the other way around?**

I'm making a trip to Florida and it's all because of the sandwich. Sandwich Generation, that is. That's the label being given to those of us who are somewhere between boomer and Gen X who are hitting middle age and coping with declining parents while we've still got kids under our roofs. Every decision I make is an attempt to balance this equation. Do I squeeze out a contribution to my retirement account this year, help pay down some of my parents' debts or keep my son from going full-on Steve Buscemi? Ultimately, I pony up for my son's braces, because no matter what career path he takes, an exploding mouthful of teeth isn't going to help him as he's already made the fatal mistake of not having been born into the top 1 percent.*

At any given moment, one of my friends might be having a sandwich. We'll be planning to get together for cocktails—after all, our kids are finally reaching the age when they should be able to spend an hour or two alone—when I'll get a call. *Ryan was trying to turn paper into parchment and almost burned the house down. We're having a family meeting, wish us luck!* Or, *Mom fell and broke her hip.* Or, *Dad had a [fill in the blank with any number of ailments] and needs a [fill in the blank with any number of procedures] and I'm flying to [fill in the blank with any number of destinations], so let's try again. How does four years from now work for you guys?* If the NSA is wiretapping our phones, sadly the only pattern of note is how often the Mayo Clinic comes up in conversations.

We're the meat. You want to get to the meat, but before you do, you have to chew through the bread. An indication of how much things have changed in the last few years is that I used to look forward to going to Miami for a very different kind of sandwich— a Cuban sandwich. Ham and slow-roasted pork smothered in melted cheese on grilled bread. At my age, I shouldn't be indulging in this cholesterol festival, but I'll need at least one of these to sustain me on this mission.

The timing is terrible. I don't believe in any kind of universal

---

*Statistics sadly report that is the most important determinant of success, though my husband and I like to say we've purposely middled out so at least he doesn't have to worry about not doing as well as us, which can be a burden, too.

law other than Randomness Happens, but it does seem like family emergencies, whopping credit card bills and bad skin always arrive at the worst possible moments. This is the second trip I will make to Florida this year. I was just there a few months ago.

The first emergency occurred before I'd had a chance to catch my breath after my son's bar mitzvah. Planning and executing a bar mitzvah is never a walk in the park, but when you're an atheist on a budget, you end up doing a lot of juggling.* There were several compelling reasons to have our son bar mitzvahed. Not only is it a time-honored tradition in our cultural, if not religious, heritage, but even more important our parents were getting so old that this could be one of the last big celebrations for their grandson they might be around to enjoy.

Complicating this plan was that we don't belong to a temple.† Luckily, I was able to arrange for my son to study with someone I'd met on a writing assignment. I'd just covered what was believed to be the first bat mitzvah in an American women's prison. It was the only time I'd been in temple where the person sitting next to me had the words SUICIDAL FREAK tattooed on her neck. There's a saying, "There are no atheists in foxholes," but it should

---

*I resent the word "juggling" almost as much as I hate the word "entitlements." As a younger person, you can find yourself happily juggling part-time jobs, relationships and belief systems. Whenever you employ the word "juggling" at this age, it's code for "things I'm failing to do well," in the same way that when politicians throw out the word "entitlements," you know the implication is "things we don't think you've earned."

†We live in a town where a service industry exists that offers friends, paparazzi and even rabbis for rent at a moment's notice, but a work-for-hire spiritual leader might be a red flag. One can only hope that the same people available as instant paparazzi aren't also the same ones who can bar mitzvah you.

. . . . . .

be amended to add ". . . or in penitentiaries."* If I am ever incarcerated you can bet I'll be signing up for every form of religious education offered. They have the best snacks; they observe holidays and often meet in air-conditioned halls. I figured if that rabbi could handle lifers, he could do just fine with my teenager.

But where to hold the event? Our home, with its temperamental seventy-year-old plumbing, is not ideal. As the rabbi's congregation meets in a double-wide trailer on the grounds of the California Institution for Women in Chino, his place wasn't an option. Ultimately, we were offered a meeting room at my son's Episcopal elementary school. It was their first and I believe only bar mitzvah to date.

Being an atheist had never stopped me from enjoying the ritual, community singing, gay friendly and general do-unto-others-as-you-would-have-them-do-unto-you sentiment of the school's chapel services, plus, the school had amazing camping trips. A camping trip that includes margaritas? What's not to like? My son and I had also spent numerous Friday nights volunteering in the church's soup kitchen, so to have the ceremony in that space seemed ideal.

The administration apparently wasn't holding it against us that Ezra held the distinction of being the only kid to ever refuse participation in the annual kindergarten Christmas pageant. It wasn't the message of the play he objected to, it was his role that he took issue with. He was assigned to be an angel while he envi-

---

*There is a prominent humanist organization in the military now, Atheists in Foxholes, but I'm not sure about the quality of their snacks.

. . . . . .

sioned himself a shepherd. If you saw my round-faced, golden-locked cherub at that age, *you* would have cast him as an angel. People used to stop us on the street and say, "Your kid would have gotten a lot of work in Michelangelo's time." He looked like he'd floated down from the roof of the Sistine Chapel. Normally, I wouldn't have indulged this kind of behavior, but before I had a chance to intervene, his teacher had brokered a deal with him. As long as he agreed not to recruit other recalcitrant angels into his boycott and faithfully (as it were) attend rehearsals, he could recuse himself from the performance. That he kept his end of the bargain exhibited a certain maturity that I had to admire. Even during the play, when I whispered, "Don't you miss singing with your friends?" he remained firm and stated, "I'm singing along in my head." I had to give it to him.

The bar mitzvah went off with just a few minor glitches. The only accommodation the rabbi had requested was that any crucifixes be removed or covered during the ceremony, something the church officials were kind enough to agree to. It wasn't until the service was under way that my husband and I noticed our goof. We'd inadvertently placed him and our son in front of glass windows perfectly framing them between the two life-sized statues of Jesus in the courtyard garden. Thankfully, no one pointed it out to him, and I thought it made an unusually ecumenical triptych.

Nevertheless, our parents were all in attendance. Jewish celebrations entail a rigorous coordination of meals that typically follows this progression: just a nibble of something light, breakfast, brunch, afternoon snack, something to hold you over until later, early dinner, low-blood-sugar pick-me-up, dinner, supper, something to tide you over until breakfast, and a midnight snack. Repeat until completely satiated, exhausted or bloated. We'd barely seen everyone off to their respective time zones when I got the news that my parents urgently needed to sell their home and needed assistance.

As I travel over the causeway spanning Biscayne Bay connecting Miami to my parent's home on Sunset Island II, I look out over the water at this view that was captured in the final frames of *Midnight Cowboy*. When Dustin Hoffman takes his last breath, you can see the island where my parents have resided for forty years in the background. No one is dying, but my parents are taking this move hard. My sister and I have urged them for at least the last fifteen years to sell this house. The roof tiles are cracked and leaky, the kitchen woefully outdated, property taxes exorbitant and the landscaping expensive to keep up, especially when hurricanes regularly fell trees. But for my parents, the island itself had become part of their identity. It was an address that conferred status. Our neighbors once included William Paley, Howard Hughes and deposed dictator Anastasio Somoza Debayle of Nicaragua. Current residents count Anna Kournikova, Enrique Iglesias and Lenny Kravitz among their illustrious ranks. I am convinced a move will be good for our parents. The equity from the sale of the house should provide money to live on, plus they've grown isolated on the island. Many of the newer islanders come for only brief visits and the absence of other year-rounders is palpable. Entire blocks of houses are dark for months at a time. My parents have also taken to keeping their cumbersome storm

......

shutters up all year round. It's making their home seem like a mausoleum. A change of scenery might do them good, but this move will mark their entry into the next and probably last chapter of their lives. My parents have been supportive grandparents, showing up for baseball games and music recitals, making valiant attempts to keep current with newfangled distractions. "What's this about Ezra and his Vines? He's into horticulture now?" It's heartbreaking to witness this passage.*

I arrive to find my mother in a state of high anxiety. The house sold within weeks of listing it on the market and they are completely unprepared. My mother is intent on getting rid of everything she owns; if I'd shown up any later, my parents might be sleeping on tatami mats. She's always had an eye for bargains and has already had an auction house cart away the items she acquired at thrift shops and estate sales that are now worth much more than she paid. Lamps, silk oriental rugs, a silver-plated tea service, a piano, and even the majority of their tables and chairs. The house has been eerily emptied out. Luckily, the time has passed when her possessions held an appeal for me, as it's come to my attention that my own furniture is aging me. Having a house full of antiques can seem winningly eccentric when you're young, but just the other day I caught sight of myself in a mirror sitting in a rocker from the 1930s and wondered what Grandma Moses was doing hanging out in my living room. Wearing vintage clothes

---

*The day my son introduced me to six-second Vines as "the most entertaining things in the world" was when I started pricing llama farms.

when you *are* vintage is a double negative. The last thing I need is more old-timey ephemera, but I feel something I might even call grief in the pit of my stomach.

My mother ushers me into the garage, where card tables are piled with items she wants to pass on to me. It's the kind of clutter the *Grey Gardens* set designer might have culled to re-create the dilapidated home of Big and Little Edie.

Of the objects I can identify, there are chipped dishes and bowls, moldy books and a miniature scales of justice, something everyone's dad had on his desk in the seventies.

Then there is the memorabilia from my father's many businesses. As a serial entrepreneur, his career spanned a wide range of industries. There's a six-foot-long historical drawing of St. Louis Union Station in Saint Louis, from his noble but unrealized attempt to restore the historic landmark. I'm tempted to rescue it, but it's been neglected for so long the print is yellowed, frayed and covered in watermarks. There's a poster for a film called *The Silent Partner*, which I'm surprised to see because it dates from the foray into soft-core porn distribution that ended disastrously. His company released such classics as *Poor White Trash*, also known as *Scum of the Earth* and *The Naked Rider*. One of my fondest childhood memories is reciting *Naked Rider*'s radio ads: *In the house she was a lady, but in the stable, she was*—horse neighing sound—*an animal.* The one film that had some artistic value, *The Silent Partner*, starring Christopher Plummer, tanked, sending the company into the Chapter Eleven that marked the end of my college education. There are a few lithographs, also

. . . . . .

very degraded, that might be from his gallery. Yes, there was an art gallery as well. There was a travel agency, a silver mine and a door factory. A high point was the period during which he and a partner owned The Embers, a much-beloved classic steak house that had fallen into disrepair. The restaurant was a Miami Beach institution, famous for its fire pit, thick-cut steaks, potatoes au gratin and baked apples. Ever the ham, I was thrilled to perform a few songs for his reopening of the restaurant. When your business partner goes by the single nickname "Blackie," you might suspect mob connections. During those years, I was my father's confidante. I was a senior in high school when he was offered a brown paper bag containing $50K in return for laundering money. "Do it," I advised, calculating the cost of the double perm I was longing to ruin my already frizzy hair with. He declined, but it was not uncommon to hear that business associates or close friends were heading off to serve time in white-collar prisons. The restaurant closed its doors within eighteen months. Not long after, I was cast as a hooker who was being harassed by her pimp, Choo Choo, in *Miami Vice*. Wouldn't you know it, my character operated her business out of The Embers, which was now a Euro-trash hotspot. Dad has no emotional attachment to any of this stuff, as he bequeathed his "legacy gift" to us years ago. During a visit to Florida, I found my father and five-year-old son sitting together on the floor. "Grandpa is teaching me how to play craps," my son told me excitedly, holding up my father's set of ivory dice, though his "never say die" resiliency is without a doubt the most valuable gift he's passed on to us.

That feeling in my stomach is growing into something I might

. . . .

call despair, but what can I do with this stuff? The tradition of preserving family heirlooms, such as they are, is something likely to disappear in the coming years. I can't imagine my son, a citizen of the digital age, will either have room for or want to keep the photographs of relatives whose names have been forgotten, not to mention the other crap I've acquired over the years. *Must do a major purge when I get home,* I tell myself as my mother and I pack up boxes for either Goodwill or the large dumpster we've rented.*

The object I feel the most affection for turns out to be a brass ashtray from the seventies. It still has ashes in it. Either they've never cleaned it or someone is still smoking. I don't ask. I shove the ashtray, ashes and all, into a brown paper bag to take home with me.

I spend several heated hours convincing my mother not to get rid of her dining room furniture. Even though we've yet to determine where they'll be heading, I tell her it's safe to assume that they won't be living in a yurt and will still need a surface to eat off of and something to sit on.

My parents are completely flummoxed by small details. How do we get the gas turned off? How will we get electricity turned on when we find a new place? How do we get new phone numbers and how will our Social Security checks find us when we get to wherever it is that we're going? It frightens me to think of them continuing to live on their own. If they don't know these things,

---

*I've been holding on to my Steely Dan and Crosby, Stills and Nash 8-tracks, thinking they might make a comeback someday. Last time I checked eBay, 8-tracks were listing for $6.50. I should have saved the vinyl. Wrong again!

. . . . . .

how have they been managing their day-to-day affairs and what else are they unsure of that I don't know about?

While I'm there, we learn that a condo located nearby has become available for a short-term rental. Even though we still don't know what they can actually afford as none of their finances are in order, they must vacate the house, so my sister and I advise them to take it. My parents react as though we're shipping them off to a senior internment camp. Mom suggests it might be easier if we just leave them on the side of a mountaintop.

My mother would prefer to be working. She was forcibly retired at seventy-four from a job she'd gotten ten years prior, despite stellar job reviews, to make way for younger employees. You're living longer, so you want to work longer, but that just edges out younger people from the workforce, so the only thing that makes sense is that we need to extend childhood. I suck at math, but if you take all the metrics into account, my son should still be in diapers.*

Each day I make phone calls to utility companies, but if I leave the house for even an hour, I return to find my parents have undone the work I've just completed. It's impossible to convince my parents that they can retain their email addresses. "Dad, your email address has nothing to do with your modem," I tell him. Even my father, who has always been an early adopter, is stumped. "Email comes in through the computer, which is connected to the modem, which farms it out to your phone."

----

*In Western Europe, the decline of the euro is likely to push the retirement age to between seventy and eighty, and to think, only a few years ago, Greece was an ideal place to retire.

"How can it possibly work that way? What if you're not near the modem when you get your emails? What about people who don't own a computer and only have smartphones?" But it's no use. I arrange new phone numbers for them as well, but by the time I arrive back in Los Angeles I learn they've jettisoned them even though I'd already distributed the new ones to our family members and all of their medical providers. And these are the same people some politicians claim would benefit from privatized retirement accounts and a health-care voucher system. If I wasn't convinced of this already, I know these things are all code for "more things my sister and I will need to do for our parents."

I can only hope that my son, who already programs my iPod, will have more patience when he has to do something similar for me. "Mom, the chip embedded in your thumb doesn't need to be reprogrammed when you move!" Where will I be headed when that day comes? With my lackluster savings, it will probably be an elder hostel in Costa Rica.

It's only as I am packing to leave Miami that I fully take in that this is the last time I'll be in my childhood home. I too had relished this fancy address, and the feeling in the pit of my stomach has turned to anguish. I frantically call the real estate agent to ask if I can keep the brass knocker on the front door. This fixture, a realistically carved, delicate woman's hand whose nails I once painted black, had always been vaguely disturbing to me in the way that a disembodied limb can seem to a child, but now I want to hold that hand. Alas, I am told the new owners find the knocker endearingly kitsch, and so I shake that hand good-bye forever. I've got my dirty ashtray in my purse as I roll my overnight bag

. . . . . .

over the pale coral stone walkway and I can still make out the red wax candle drippings from my *Rocky Horror Picture Show* party that even repeated steam cleanings couldn't erase. But there's no time to mourn because my son's heading toward his first day of his last year in middle school and I've got back-to-school shopping to do.

My list of back-to-school supplies includes wipe boards and corkboards. These "organizational tools" continue to pile up and go unused in our house, but every year I convince myself that this new chart of chores, fresh calendars hung in every room, and homework or musical instrument practice check-off sheets will finally make our household run smoothly. No matter what kind of new system I try to implement, my son makes last-minute plans and mixes up important dates, but I can't resist, and so I'm loading bigger corkboards and brighter dry-erase markers into a shopping cart, as if a reminder in lime green of *Write down dates of upcoming tests!* will make a deeper impression than the ones I've previously written in black, when the phone rings. It's my older sister with news. This is how the communication chain works. Even though I'm nearing fifty, I'm still the younger sibling. She gets the important news from our parents and is called upon to break it to me.

There's good news and bad news. The bad news is that my mother has breast cancer again. The (relatively) good news is that she's so old the cells aren't growing quickly and her oncologist is confident that a radical mastectomy should take care of it.

The news about her breast cancer shouldn't be shocking. In the last hundred years, we've doubled our life span as Americans, but our "lengthening morbidity," as it's been called, is both enervating and expensive, with many of us outliving the money it costs to treat these diseases.* She's had breast cancer once already and made it through with only a short course of radiation, but she's had thyroid cancer and had her thyroid removed as well. She had a benign brain tumor removed with no lasting repercussions other than her sticking with the Rod Stewart circa 1982 haircut she adopted in preparation for that surgery. We've nicknamed my mother the Energizer Bunny because she just keeps going and going, but how long can she last?

I volunteer to go back down for the surgery and spend the night in the hospital with my mother, like I did when she had the brain tumor. Ever since the birth of my son with a congenital birth defect necessitating years of surgical repair—all successful, I am happy to report—I am the go-to person in the family when it comes to health care. My executive-decision-making older sister handles financial, legal and much of their emotional support— she's a rock—but health crisis management has become my domain.† I really have no expertise, but I have learned a few simple tricks. Write down everything your doctor says. Write down every medication you are already taking, every medication you will need during your recovery and every question you can think of. Keep an extra pen on you; yours will run out of ink when you need it the most. And whenever possible, find someone to stay with you overnight. Anyone will do. Pay someone if necessary.

---

* "Lengthening morbidity" has a catchy ring to it, no? No. It does not.
† This division of labor never fails to remind me of how I've failed my own son by not having other siblings to share the responsibilities one day.

You won't regret it. The night shift is hard, nurses are overworked and often the medications and orders are confusing, so be nice to them. And BYO pillow, bathrobe, socks and blanket for both patient and caregiver.

My mother finds it comforting that her oncologist is someone I went to high school with, whom I may or may not have dated. I actually can't remember. Since her retirement, her life has compressed to the point that her relationships with her doctors are primary and deeply personal. She's sounding more and more like my grandmother Rebecca, who sent cards to her doctors on their birthdays and regularly hand-delivered homemade banana bread and stuffed cabbage to their offices. This must be another milestone that lies ahead for me: the day when you speak to and of your doctors more frequently than your friends. All of this is made even more surreal by the fact that the person my mother now wants to send pastries to (store-bought, but still) is someone my age.

As her surgery looms closer, I find myself feeling sentimentally attached to my mom's breast. It makes no sense. Like many people my age, I wasn't breast-fed, nor have I been particularly close with my mother for most of my life, but I am mourning the loss of this body part, maybe more than she. She is approaching the surgery with a very practical attitude. "I'm not using it anymore," she tells me. Bit by bit, I am losing parts of my mother, and I am tempted to call her doctor and ask if I can preserve her breast, like a relic, in one of the pricey BPA-free glass containers I've invested in so my son won't have plastic leaching into his body.

. . . .

When she announces she doesn't want to have an implant, my sister and I phone her together to make sure she's thought through her decision thoroughly. We're concerned it might affect her self-esteem, but she's worried about the safety and the longevity of implants.

"You're seventy-seven," I remind her. "You probably only need it to last for ten years at the most. If you're worried about leakage, I've got these inserts shaped like chicken cutlets; I used to put them in my bra for auditions that call for cleavage." I have no idea what they're made of, but they're very durable. I've had the same set for fifteen years. "We could ask your doctor if we can just stick those in there." That's when she reminds us that she will need only one.

We're stumped. None of us know if there are implants on the market that will mirror my mother's remaining seventy-seven-year-old breast. I suggest she ask her surgeon for a marsupial pouch in which she could carry her phone, mints or that grandma standby—balled-up, slightly used tissues.

"I've got a few old cashmere sweaters," I offer. "They're so soft and probably the right consistency; they used to make them with such tight weave. What about a chunk of my Tempur-Pedic pillow? It really does mold to any shape you want."

I remind her that having only one breast can cause an imbalance in equilibrium. Walking down the street with my mother is already dangerous. She tends to veer slightly and has a lot of pent-up frustration. I worry she might steer my father, who has begun to shuffle ever so slightly, into oncoming traffic either on purpose or by accident. But she's having none of it.

. . . . . .

I See You Made an Effort

I arrive the night before the surgery. It will be the first time I will visit them since they've left our old home. I pull up to the condo and see that the building is situated right on the beach, convenient for healthful, invigorating walks. I'd hoped that wherever they landed, they'd meet new people. As I head inside I discover that each wing of the building has its own elevator, a luxury feature that is intended to make the building seem exclusive, but it has the opposite effect of what I was hoping for them. The elevator opens right at their front door. They share this elevator with only a small number of tenants, who live on floors directly above and below them. During my stay, I see no one else in the building except the staff and learn that my parents haven't been strolling along the water either. They've arranged the furniture in an identical configuration as it was in their home and, because they feel the place gets too much light, they keep the curtains closed. They've completely re-created their old home, right up to the lack of a view.

I get no sleep the night before the surgery because I'm still on Los Angeles time and my husband and I need to coordinate a new carpool, music lesson and sports practice schedule. This process is made slower because my parents can't figure out how to access their new Internet service. They tell me their password is the address of the old house, but they can't remember what they've named their wireless connection. I try dozens of combinations of passwords and network names and they pull out service manuals they've taken to their new residence where they think they've written down the codes, but none of them are correct. In addition,

......

the service manuals are for electronics they no longer own: a Betamax, an answering machine and a slide projector. I can't get online and am slowly texting times and dates until it's time we take my mother to the hospital for her early morning pre-op intake process.

Everyone who greets us at the hospital, from the surgeon to the administrative staff, is extremely courteous and helpful. "Say something funny," Juan, the young orderly, says when he hears I work in comedy, as he wheels my mother into the pre-op room. My mom is chattering on and on about relatives who are no longer alive, relatives she is no longer in touch with and relatives who are no longer in their right minds. She's nervous. Juan looks at me expectantly. "My mom's brain surgery was easier to deal with— she was sedated longer," I say. The hallway at Mount Sinai Hospital is a tough room.

While my mother is in surgery I stop into the cafeteria for my Cuban sandwich and a café con leche and run into the wife of the homecoming king of my high school class. We've kept loosely in touch through social media, but we're not close enough for me to have known that our former monarch is in the hospital, too. When she tells me this news, there's the briefest pause in our conversation. She doesn't tell me what he's doing there, and I don't ask. I know this is how it will be from now on: if someone doesn't offer, you don't ask.

It's startling how quickly the surgery is over and Mom is assigned a room. Waiting for her to rouse, I see that she's got a bay view; in fact, we can see Sunset Island II just across the water.

. . . . . .

We're less than two miles from our old house. I know I must be really tired, because I'm entertaining the notion that this whole surgery was just an attempt to get closer to the island. But as soon as she wakes up it's clear that she's headed for a quick recovery, because she's already complaining about how slow the nurses are.

Before we're allowed to leave the hospital, a nurse instructs me on how to manage the drainage tubes that collect the bloody discharge from the incision, a process technically referred to as "milking."* I'm so glad I'm the mother of a teenager. I've taken my son to see enough vampire flicks that the sight of blood doesn't faze me a bit, thank you, Stephenie Meyer. You squeeze the blood down through the tubes, inch by inch, until it collects into a bulbous container, and then you empty the liquid from the bulb. Repeat every few hours. Each time I do this, my mother gazes at me with the wide-eyed expectancy of a toddler on the first snow day of the year. Socks, underpants, long underwear, sweater, snow bib, parka, boots, mittens, scarf, earmuffs. "Now let's put your hood on. Good girl!" It's a lugubrious process made even slower by the antediluvian equipment. The nurse asks us if we've got any safety pins. "No." She shakes her head as if everyone carries safety pins with them at all times. "No one said anything about safety pins," I say, my practiced hospital patience beginning to wane. It takes three different nurses to locate two safety pins. Once we've been sufficiently chastised, our nurse shows us

---

*It's really horrible that women who've just lost a breast have to then learn how to "milk" the drainage. Couldn't they think of a name for this without the sorrowful connotation?

how we'll be pinning these bloody bulbs inside my mother's blouses while she heals. How is it possible that we can collect energy from the sun through photovoltaic panels, but we can't collect blood except with a jerry-rigged contraption that includes safety pins?

At ten p.m. we're told she'll be going home the next day. That's when I get the brilliant idea that I might be able to make it back to Los Angeles in time to accompany my son to Fuck Yeah Fest, the indie rock festival he's been pining to attend. He's planning on meeting up with several girls who are going to be there. I've been read the riot act. I am to accompany him to the festival grounds and disappear from sight, dissolve into the ether, if possible, until he's ready to go home. "So, is there someone you like?"

"I just want to make out with girls."

"Anyone in particular?"

"No, Mom, any girls." I have found a purpose in my son's life. This will mark my new incarnation as a wingmom. So with the help of more of that local café con leche, I pull another all-nighter. I purchase concert tickets online and begin making lists of after-care procedures for my sister, who is scheduled to fly in and take over after my departure. I've collected times and dates of support groups for cancer patients, meditation classes for cancer patients, yoga for cancer patients, bra fittings for cancer patients—there are even makeover days for cancer patients. With one out of eight women in the U.S. being diagnosed with breast cancer, the related industries are so extensive, I almost expected to find a service providing cancer for cancer patients. I record the contact numbers for mom's doctors and home health-care provider, plus an admonition to make sure to have extra safety pins on hand as well.*

By the next afternoon, we've gotten my mother home, and by the evening I feel satisfied that she can perform her own milking and has the meds she needs, at least until my sister arrives. I beg my parents to open the curtains once a day, knowing full well that they won't, and I head to the airport to catch the last flight of the day out of town.

My plane lands at midnight. After stopping for gas, I accidentally drive over a small concrete island and knock off one of my hubcaps, but my mother just had a boob lopped off, so I'm able to shrug that off without too much fuss.

A few hours into the next day, my son and I head to the festival grounds located in an industrial area on the outskirts of Los Angeles. It's dusty, loud and 102 degrees. It takes us over an hour to snake through the long line of teenagers until we make it to the entrance, only to find out that in my exhaustion I bought tickets for the wrong day.

"Please, please, let us use these tickets today," I beg the security person but he's not budging. "Do I look like I'm trying to sneak into this concert?"

"You'll have to come back tomorrow, ma'am."

"That's right, I *am* a ma'am and you couldn't pay me to come back tomorrow." My son is mortified and moves several feet away from me. He wants nothing to do with me. I have not only screwed

---

*I have since found some drainage systems do come equipped with clips. I'm not crafty but it seems like a wound care system that requires sharp pins operated by someone who just had surgery and is on strong painkillers is a design failure.

. . . . . .

up with the tickets but also in doing so, totally lost any sliver of credibility I might have had in the ongoing campaign to get us organized at home.

I get the silent treatment until I agree to drop him off alone at the fairgrounds the next day, something I consent to because by this point, I've only got the briefest connection left to my sanity. As I speed away from the concert grounds I pass a billboard with the alarming sentiment "Prepare for a Longer Retirement," writ large. I turn on the radio just in time to hear that suicides, formerly the domain of disaffected teenagers and depressed seniors, are suddenly on the rise for boomers and researchers aren't sure why. Ask me. I know why! It's a miracle that billboard alone isn't sending drivers careening off the roads lemming-style.* During what seems to be an interminable drive home, I remember that I've left my phone charger and night guard on the plane.

But there's no time to dwell because I'm going to be needed for the next emergency soon enough. And wouldn't you know it, this whole episode has left me with a whopping credit card bill; between the last-minute plane tickets, the misplaced dental appliance and the concert debacle, I've spent over a thousand dollars in the last two days, and I've got a big honking pimple on my chin.

---

*An American turns fifty every seven seconds—that's nearly 12,500 each day. If I were really paranoid, I might consider that the billboard was erected for just that purpose, as a ploy to keep Social Security solvent.

. . . . . .

SAVES

Dear God,

Forgive me, Father, for I have Googled. I have Googled the Mayo Clinic, WebMD, and even Yahoo! Answers.

Googling health problems on the Internet is normally a bad idea, but at forty-nine, it's a disastrous mistake. Any ache or pain can be linked to an impressive number of horrifying age-related conditions. From what I could deduce this time, I appeared to be suffering from a degenerative form of arthritis and Heberden's nodes, also known in colloquial terms as old-lady hands. Fucking fifty.

It was an early Monday morning in October, one month before my fiftieth birthday, when I awoke with the certainty that a substantial percentage of the twelve million cars that travel the Los Angeles freeway daily had spent the night driving back and forth over my hands. The little finger on my left hand appeared to be crooked, and a bump on the distal interphalangeal joint (that's the middle one) of my right forefinger was swollen. Any movement was agonizing. My neck was also slightly compressed. I use the word "slightly" because my skull has never actually been clamped into a vise, and I imagine that a vise might be preferable to the electric pain shooting through my head. It took bed rest and continuous hot packs to get through the day while consulting Dr. Google for what my husband speculated was a case of exacerbated bone spurs and a sore neck.

"It seems like the exertion of putting together your son's trampoline has activated a genetic predisposition for osteoarthritis in your neck," pronounced the rheumatologist I begrudgingly went to see.

"What about this?" I asked and held out my hands.

"Oh, we just call that old-lady hands."

As someone who loves being right, this was one time when it just plain sucked. I had just described how I'd single-handedly assembled a twelve-foot trampoline for my son, jumped on it for a few hours, and now couldn't button my blouse. The Skywalker 2000 came unassembled with maybe ninety-odd pieces and presented an irresistible challenge because I pride myself on my prowess with a power tool. I have half-painted furniture and bedroom walls scarred by poorly executed attempts to mount pictures, but a self-contained project can be satisfying, even if done poorly. Following a set of rules is relaxing, an antidote to a career as a freelancer in which there is always more to be done. Perhaps women in earlier centuries felt that way about lacing up a corset;

it gave shape to your day in addition to your waistline. It took me only three and a half hours of straining to fasten the springs into the frame, with only two hopefully unimportant screws and one large piece of metal tubing to spare.

That first day, my son invited friends over and jumped for hours. When the boys left, I decided to give it a try. I had been warned that for anyone who has given birth and not done Kegels religiously—and by religiously, I mean continuously from the moment you give birth—leakage is to be expected. I hadn't been on a trampoline in more than thirty years and in those first jumps, two sensations surged through my body: complete happiness and the jolt of something becoming dislodged internally. Thank goodness I had on dark jeans. I jumped for two exhilarating hours.

Undressing that night, I found an even bigger surprise than I realized. It had taken only one day of trampolining to return my period to me. I've still got it, I told myself. I'm not really old yet. I could still have a baby. A baby with a one-in-ten chance of severe birth defects, but I could do it. Not that I wanted a baby, but I could still have one. Still fertile. Fuck you, fifty, I'm still young! The door that slammed shut with menopause had creaked back open.

The sheer joy of jumping made me feel invincible. Having stumbled upon something so unexpected and fantastic, I went to sleep feeling that anything was possible. Our trampoline was, if not a fountain of youth, the closest thing to it you can purchase without a prescription. At least for the sum of three hundred dollars, which is only a hundred and ninety dollars more than an ounce of Hope in a Jar miracle moisturizing cream. Of course, I hadn't figured in the cost of a doctor's visit, and now this doctor was telling me I'd caused irreversible damage, and that could mean only one thing: staggeringly high medical bills.

As Dr. Nudgey droned on, I considered which word was less sexy, "arthritis" or "rheumatology," and decided it was a draw.

Nudgey, I concluded, had the worst bedside manner in the world, when he added, "You're my youngest patient." Why the need to tell me that? At various points in my life I had hoped to be the youngest person to win an Academy Award, a Pulitzer Prize, a MacArthur Genius, but I never, ever wanted to be the youngest patient of a doctor who treats persons afflicted with aging-related diseases.* I was dabbing at my eyes as the doctor, who was ancient himself, told me that I should put it in perspective.

"You don't have pancreatic cancer."

"Yes, I know that," I said without mentioning that my old-lady hands had recently helped one of my best friends with that exact disease to exit this world.

"That's one of the . . ."

"Bad cancers," I said, thinking how nice it would be to have a numbing dosage of OxyContin right about now.

"I have high blood pressure and a low-functioning thyroid; that's worse, let me tell you."

Were we in a disease-off?

Then he told me how his own mother tried to warn him of the horrors of aging, telling him, "You'll see," every time he ques-

---

*One of the first telltale signs of aging might be noticing that you've started rooting for the oldest athletes in any given league. I'm holding out hope that Martina Navratilova will come out of retirement.

tioned her lifestyle: "Mom, why don't you get out of your bathrobe during the day?" "You'll see." "Mom, why don't you take an exercise class?" "You'll see." He tells me there is really nothing I can do.

"I've read about glucosamine and chondroitin. What about taking those?"

"They don't really work."

"Exercise?"

"Doesn't work."

"Changing my diet?"

"Nope."

"Acupuncture?"

"You can go ahead and spend money on that if you want to, but it doesn't do any good."

I wanted to take my old-lady hands, put them around his neck and strangle him.

Dr. Nudgey did suggest one course of action. "You can down fistfuls of aspirin, but that's about it. There's no cure, and it only gets worse."

That's when the weeping began.

He asked me if my mother had disfigured hands. "No," I replied, but then I thought about my grandmother Frances. She'd had knobby fingers for as long as I could remember. I assumed this was the result of her meticulous cleaning. She washed the wallpaper in her dining room so often that the glue seeped through. When my cousins and I would slap our artwork and spelling tests against the wall, they stuck. She even had wheels

. . . . . .

put on her larger pieces of furniture to make polishing the floor easier.

Just when I'd gotten used to the idea that my once smooth hands were becoming as veiny as my mother's, I was going straight for gnarly grandma hands. Frances, whose character had been shaped by the Depression, never complained about pain in her hands, thus leaving me totally unprepared. I'd also used Frances's hands as an excuse for my poor housekeeping skills, and now I'd have no excuse.*

Maybe the weeping got to Dr. Nudgey, because he thrust some informational pamphlets at me, said he was going to write up his notes and hurriedly exited the examination room.

The pamphlets highlighting gadgets specifically designed for osteoarthritis sufferers were even more depressing than Nudgey's bedside manner. Jar openers, button and zipper pulls, playing-card holders and, yes, even walkers. Each item was offered in a variety of rainbow hues.

I mark this day as my first experience with how the elderly are infantilized. The faces of the people in the pamphlets appeared vaguely distorted, their bodies rounded like Botero sculptures. Has this condition rendered them incapable of exercise, trans-forming them into sexless, shapeless blobs? These rotund couples were dressed in those same insipid pastel-colored sweaters as the AARP elders. The dreaded, neutering pleated khakis were boxy

---

*There were signs. I inherited a large collection of gloves. A younger person as-sumes a fondness for phalangeal accessorizing. Now It All Makes Sense.

to boot. My son was right: khaki hadn't murdered anyone, but it was almost as bad, and the pants were so high-waisted they looked like geriatric rompers. Each couple was depicted at home. Was it by accident or by design that their homes were isolated structures? Shunned by society, had they been cast out to dwell on the fringes of civilization? In one drawing, a woman is tossing a salad with gigantic pink tongs under a man's watchful eye. Which one has the osteoarthritis? Is it the woman wielding the circus-clown utensils, or the man, so handicapped he's unable to lift the massive tongs? It's probably both of them. The disease has turned him into a mercurial taskmaster, and he's overseeing the preparations, making sure she tosses the salad with flavored water to keep their weight down.

I gazed expectantly toward the bank of windows located just above my head. They don't open. Given Dr. Nudgey's winning personality, it's possible that the building's management has sealed them as a precautionary measure.

I'd worked myself into a total panic by the time Dr. Nudgey came back. He took in the sight of me still weeping, and said to make an appointment to see him again in six months. Why on earth would I do that? So I could come back and he could make me feel worse?

"No, thank you, that won't be necessary," I said as I squeezed the door handle with my better hand, exited and didn't look back.

When I arrived home, my son was jumping on the tramp. The 2000 doesn't much resemble the trampolines I grew up with. Those had menacingly large, exposed industrial-sized metal springs. The springs looked like sharks' teeth to me. You could land on them and chip a tooth or fall through the gaping spaces between each one. At the summer camps I attended, we were made to stand shoulder to shoulder as safety watch whenever another kid was jumping. We were ordered to be vigilant. The extent of this danger was constantly drilled into our heads. "Don't turn away for a second, not a second! Donna Rosenstock broke her collarbone last June! She's still in a neck brace!"

Now trampoline springs are covered by protective plastic sheeting, and ours even came with netting that encloses the tarp so the whole thing resembles a giant playpen. Should a bounce threaten to send you sailing over the edge, the net catches you and gently rights you. It's not unlike the evolution of childhood itself. We keep our children corralled in our homes or backyards, and when we do let them venture out, we arm them with cell phones, yet another layer of netting.*

"Come on with me, Mom."

"No, my hands hurt, I can't," I said as I watched him jump into the evening hours from the kitchen breakfast-nook window. My son was actually asking me to do something with him, but I was too defeated to join him.

"Are your bones brittle because you're soooooo old?"

Art Linkletter was right. Kids do say the darnedest things. I headed straight to my closet and put on my darkest pair of jeans.

We're on the trampoline. We've brought a small beach ball

---

*We sent our son to a sleepaway camp that posted photographs of the campers on-line daily. I was appalled—camp had been my annual refuge from my parents—but I couldn't help myself, I checked the site every single night during the entire two weeks he attended. Some days I checked it twice.

. . . . . .

inside the netting and we're passing it back and forth while we're jumping. It's hard to time it right between bounces, so there's a lot of careening around. Every few bounces, Ezra deliberately propels himself through the air into the net, which ricochets his slender frame back onto the tarp. He rubs his bony legs and then springs back up as if nothing has happened. I marvel at his flexibility. You'd never know that he was born with a tethered spinal cord. The memory of his reconstructive surgery, at age four, is inaccessible to him but in yet one more reminder of the effect of aging on the brain, that incident remains as vivid for me as if it had taken place yesterday, while I have no recollection of whether it was ibuprofen or acetaminophen that Nudgey advised me to take an hour earlier.

He tells me he's got a game he devised with his friends; he's named it "Saves."

"So you have to keep the ball in the air," he explains, "and to score a point you have to save it from falling by catching it," but for some reason I can't understand what he's saying. *What's the point of the game?* I'm wondering. *Are we trying to keep a volley going, or prevent the other person from hitting it back by catching the ball?* I suspect that somehow the rules conflict, but I know if I bring this up I'll be accused of correcting him. So I just nod and try to make contact with the ball while he castigates me.

"Why did you hit it like that?

"Why don't you catch it like this?

"Why aren't you trying, Mom? You're not even trying, why aren't you saving it, Mom?"

He reiterates the rules and my brain fogs over as I try to comprehend, but there are new wrinkles. "If the ball bounces once, it's a save, or if you hit it twice in the air and it touches the net, it's a save, but if it's too close to you and you catch it, it doesn't count." I'm alternating between hitting the ball and catching the ball and we're bouncing in circles around and around and maybe the bouncing has loosened something in my brain, because that's when I start to laugh.

I start to giggle and I then can't stop. I'm laughing so hard tears are streaming down my face. "Mom, stop it, stop it, Mom." But I can't. "Why are you laughing?" he demands. I can't tell him that I know I'll never ever win this game, that I can't follow the rules he's made up, that I will definitely need a massage, if not a Xanax, to correct the damage being caused right now, and that with every jump I am moving one step closer to those cartoon-sized kitchen utensils.

I can't tell him that I am trying and that sucking is the best I can do and that my inability to "save" is because I'm forty-nine years old and I'm on my way out of this life and he's on his way in. You can't tell children this. Children don't want to know this, and even if you said it, they'd never believe it and they probably couldn't hear it because it's like a high-pitched dog whistle that only people over forty can hear. I'd be his Dr. Nudgey. I don't want to be another person saying that youth is wasted on the young and that in its absence you will long for it, like someone you had great sex with but couldn't wait to leave because you had nothing to talk about. Or that you knew you were on borrowed time and it was wrong to be using someone like that, but that thing he did when you rode him backward and he'd slide his thumb inside you was truly inspired. That you had to break it off, even if there were a few slips where you showed up in the middle of the night begging him to do that thing just one more time, because it was going nowhere and you felt guilty when you were with him, but even that didn't stop you from missing him. No. I most definitely can't put it like that. I'm laughing instead.

"Why does it bother you that I'm laughing?" I ask between snorting giggles.

"You're making fun of me!"

"Oh, I'm not making fun of you." That stops my laughing cold. "That's the last thing I'm doing," I say with real compassion. But he's still mad at me and when I stumble and fall, he throws the beach ball at me and I think of the Botox I had injected into my forehead the week before. "Not the face, it's very expensive!"

"You can still win, Mom; it's only seven to minus one!"

"I can't win, Ezra, and it's okay."

"Why can't you just dive for the ball, Mom, why can't you just dive?"

That's just it. *Why* can't *I dive?* I repeat to myself as we bounce up and down, not daring to fling myself across the trampoline. It's been years since I've flung myself at something, or someone. I don't fling anymore. I've spent the last year, really the last few years, trying to feel safe, making safer choices; the last thing I want is to dive. Flinging is for the young, right? I flung myself into my career, waiting for hours in lines at cattle calls, leaving my picture and résumé under the door at casting offices up and down Seventh Avenue, dancing in the background of early MTV videos for fifty dollars cash in the hopes of being discovered. I

. . . .

dove into relationships for the most minimal reasons. Julian. His hair was dyed my favorite color of red in the eighties. I saw him riding a bike through a park in London during my study abroad summer. When I spotted him again riding through Washington Square Park in New York, that shock of stop-sign-red hair was enough to make me dive. Had I bothered to investigate a little more carefully, I would have discovered he was in high school the day we met, instead of three months into sleeping with him. That may not be the most flattering of examples, but still. I don't dive for sex after fifteen years of marriage. If our son is asleep, if the door is locked, if I haven't eaten too much for dinner, if I didn't have cheese that day, if the vibrator next to the bed has new batteries in it, then maybe.

Dive, Annabelle, dive, I tell myself. What good is it to still be here if you're not going to dive in? As I bounce higher, I think about how much I hate Anna Quindlen, her early success, her Adirondack chairs, her backyard pond and her slow-cooked stews. I've never had the patience to make a cold soup. I've had to reinvent myself professionally several times, reinvention being the last resort of people who didn't hit the jackpot in their twenties, thirties or even forties. I have an old wooden camp-style picnic table with rotting benches, and the only pond in my backyard is a green plastic ice tub that has filled with brackish water.

I switch into gear. Getting a good hate going propels me into action. *Thanks, Anna!* I dive and I'm giddy, and it's the best feeling in the world. I bounce harder and I feel like I'm drunk. I'm pacing the ring like a prizefighter that has gone too many rounds. My son says, "Mom, you look sore," and because I know him so well, I know he means "sour." He makes a face at me, but I've lost my facility of speech. I'm Raquel Welch in *One Million Years B.C.*, or Mike Tyson, and for a minute I think I could bite someone's ear off right now.

"Mom, you've got something hanging out of your nose."

"Uuurrrrrrrgggggghh!!!" A guttural shriek comes out instead of words.

"Mom, you're like an athlete now."

I want to win. It starts to drizzle and the tarp becomes slippery. I dive. The score is now seven to three. My mascara is running and drool is forming in a line down the corner of my mouth. I bounce over and push a fart out in his direction. "Mom, what are you doing? You're crazy!" My hair is matted with sweat. I'm stumbling, propelling myself across the tarp, and I'm in it to win it. But his thirteen-year-old body carries the day. It's over, and it's only when he taunts me with his win that I heave myself across the tarp and tackle him. We're wrestling, something we haven't done in years. I'm clinging to his back. I've wrapped my arms and legs tightly around him from behind.

"I still have power over you."

"No, you don't."

"Yes, I do—the power of the purse," but that doesn't make any sense to him. "I can still take you down," I growl, gripping him with a ferociousness that seems wildly inappropriate.

Even when he says, "Mom, my leg hurts," I don't believe it.

"I'm not falling for that," I say, squeezing tighter as he thrashes around on all fours.

. . . . . .

"Mom, I mean it, my leg hurts," he whimpers.

I ease up and in that brief moment he throws me off and springs to his feet. "Welcome to Loserville, loser." He laughs, and with a bounce, he's off the trampoline and heading across the lawn.

"Those were some nice saves," I hear him say as he pads inside.

"Thanks, Ezra," I yell after him.

I've deliberately farted in front of my kid. My face is a mess and I feel every one of those fifty years, and it feels kind of satisfying. I have no idea what the future looks like but I can still dive in and I intend to keep doing it.

So, fuck you, fifty, I own you. You're my bitch.

There is only one thing I know for sure. Everything is going to hurt like hell tomorrow morning.

THE FOUR A.M. CLUB

> **Dear God,**
>
> **This one's for the ladies.**

JILL:

It's not enough.

I'm not a good enough parent.

Holocaust.

I'm so sick of myself.

I hope I can fall back to sleep.

GIA:

If I could just lose these ten pounds . . . would more people come to my funeral?

MAUREEN:

I hate this pillow. . . . I also hate this pillow. . . . Why don't I have *any* good pillows?

I will probably never be able to afford to go to
Venice before it sinks forever into the water or I'll be
too old to enjoy it.

As I lie here not sleeping, I'm getting fatter.

Why didn't I take some kind of computer
programming class?

Please let me live until my kid becomes a grown-up.

My joints hurt—is that arthritis? Or cancer? Or
menopause? Or because I spent hours walking up
and down the aisles at Costco buying things I didn't
need?

What's the least amount of money I need to live on?

MAGGIE:
If I watch some porn, will my kids wake up and
walk in on me?

SUSAN:
I dream that I am looking in the mirror and notice a
couple of long chin hairs. As I look closer, it

. . . . . .

becomes dozens of really long hairs, so much so that I look like Fu Manchu. I am distressed thinking that I'd been walking around like this for who knows how long, and no one bothered to tell me. Then I come up with the idea that to spare the expense of having to get my face waxed, maybe I could just wrap it around my neck like a scarf. I wake up convinced it wasn't a dream, but reality. I have to check the mirror several times to make sure I'm not wearing a hair scarf.

CAROL:
This would be the perfect time to go through my ex-husband's phone and email.

LESLIE:
Why didn't I answer the phone and go with Michael to D.C. that weekend in 1986? If I had just answered the phone, we would have fallen in love and married, and I would have a law degree and lots of money and a husband and a great job.

Why did I have sex with John when I really didn't want to? And because I didn't really want to, does it count as cheating?

......

The Four A.M. Club

Why did I tell my professor in college that we made
hot cocoa and peppermint schnapps in our suite at
4 p.m. every day? I wanted to sound sophisticated,
but I just sounded like an idiot.

Why do I feel like I have to answer every question?
Can't I ever just say, *I don't know???* I try to come
across as smart and I end up being an asshole!

STEPHANIE:

I look at the clock and then do a countdown to when
I have to get up.

4-5-6-7-8. Four hours. Good. Get to sleep.

I get something to eat and feel horrible regret in the
a.m. when I see the empty container of almonds out
on the table.

I think about my mortality and feel nothing but my
existence and its finitude

and talk to God.

I imagine a world with no famine or mass prison
incarceration. I seek out God for unity, prayer and

. . . . . .

divine company to bridge the solitude I feel as a
singular human being.

I am an amoeba floating through the vast, infinite
inner space.

I look at the clock and then do a countdown to when
I have to get up.

5-6-7-8. Three hours. Still some time left. Get to
sleep.

AMY:
I come home from work to my family, which consists
of my husband, my teenage children and the dog.
I get the most affection from the dog.

CHRISTINE:
I wake up sweating, thinking that I forgot to put
a postage stamp on an envelope for my boss. . . .
Panic sets in. I can't sleep so I get dressed and go
to the post office and rummage through
bins of mail. I find the letter . . . with the stamp
on it.

In the morning I can't remember whether this was a dream. I spend at least an hour tracking down the mail when I get to the office.

CINDY:

I can't fall back to sleep. It's the middle of staffing season for TV writers and I am trying to get a job. I am so worried about money that I turn on the TV to distract myself. I turn on an episode of *The Waltons*. What could be more comforting and conflict-free than a soft seventies family drama? The entire episode was about how John-Boy would not make it as a writer—how it was too hard and he should basically find a new dream job. It was worse than any horror movie. Those damn sincere mountain people scared the shite out of me.

TINA:

It's too late to take an Ambien now. . . . I'll be a mess in the morning. (I should have taken it with the two glasses of wine that helped me fall asleep in the first place.)

I'm soooo hot. Get this blanket off me!

. . . . . .

Did I pay the water bill?

Did I send an invoice to my clients in the
Philippines? How much money would I need to
retire in the Philippines?

It's freezing in here!

What would I be like if I *didn't* have this hormone
patch on what was once my bikini line?

How can my boyfriend sleep so soundly?

JUDITH:
I think about what a fraud I am and what happens
when I'm found out and whom I could entrust to
take and destroy my computer in case of my
impending illness and death.

And then I play Scrabble.

BRENDA:
My mind lasers in on revising my living will's
medical directive. Since seeing the movie *Amour* I
realize I need an ironclad agreement with someone.

. . . . . .

KRISTIN:

I relive the scene when I confronted a friend who was sleeping with my husband . . . ten years ago.

MARLA:

I take my age and estimated life span and calculate how much time I have left on the planet. I try it with different combinations owing to various medical conditions, likelihood of automobile accidents and natural disasters and still get the same approximate answer—less time ahead than behind me!

Will I ever have sex again, and why would God want to limit the amount of sex I have?

I think about the wrongdoings of the traffic patrol and envision retribution for the two tickets I recently got. I could take that department down. Stage a Twitter campaign—write to John Stossel on ABC's *20/20*. He will want this story! I will become a hero to drivers nationwide.

KATHLEEN:

Why did I major in the humanities? I should have majored in the amenities.

. . . .

MEREDITH:

I'm wondering what alternatives there are to
elementary school for my kids. Wouldn't it be way
more educational and fun to travel around the world
experiencing different cultures? Then I think that's
ridiculous—too difficult, too expensive. I should
move to a farm or the mountains, where people are
less cynical, but what would I do? I would be bored
because I enjoy cynical people. Wait, I'm thinking
crazy thoughts because I'm so tired. I should try to
go back to sleep, but I'm thinking of all of the things
I have to get done and then I'm irritated because I
need to go back to sleep or I'll be a wreck and I try
to make my mind go blank. And that's when I start
playing solitaire.

MICHELLE:

I will never have hot sex again, or, let's face it, even
lame sex.

I won't remember anything funny that my kids ever
said that I didn't write down, because how could I
ever forget that?

What the hell did I eat? Because I have the most
obnoxious farts, and I fan the covers so my husband
may sleep through it and spare me the indignity.

. . . . . .

Will my kids ever aspire to more than landing a
trick on a skateboard?

ERIKA:

I obsess on the man who done me wrong. I yearn for
him. I stew over him. I imagine his head on the
pillow next to me. I see the long curve of his back, I
can hear him breathing. I imagine throwing my arm
over him and running my fingers through his chest
hair. I hear him saying, "Curl into me, baby." I can
see the crease where his bald head meets his neck
and I can smell his neck and imagine laying my lips
on his cool shoulder. I write letters to him that I will
never send. I lecture him, grab his cock, kick him
out, roll him over, cry all over him and beg him for
more psychological abuse. I'm so riled up, I stagger
over to the drawer where I keep my Ambien, bite
one in half and swallow it. As I wait for it to rescue
me, I may let my mind wander over to my empty
bank account, my empty nest, my empty bed and
the last episode of whatever TV show I'm obsessed
with, and then . . . zzzzzzzz.

JANE:

I think about living only five to ten more years and
missing Audrey's high school graduation, Ellen's

. . . . . .

first job, and not being a grandmother or being able to attend my daughters' weddings.

Was I a good mom? Was I a good wife? Why didn't I enjoy more of the small things? How do I do that now?

Why did I end up with two grade-two inoperable brain tumors? Reality sucks.

I will get through this. I can do it. I can do it.

SAMMY:

I wonder if my son will be a genius or end up in prison—because anything other than those extremes does not occur to me. I wonder about my marriage and if it is worth having one at all, even though I love my husband (mostly). I wonder if I will die before my son is old enough to not be damaged by the death of a parent—although I am seemingly in fine health. I am haunted by dying polar bears and children in Haiti to the point that I think there is something wrong with me—I mean more than the obvious.

I fantasize about what I would look like if I could afford a trainer and Botox.

I wonder about God.

ALI:

I make lists and more lists. I make lists of the lists I need to make. I combine the lists and prioritize them into one master list, but I realize I've forgotten so many things that I start the whole process all over again.

DEBBIE:

I am so fucking exhausted by my life that I sleep like a drunken whore.

Acknowledgments

Every writer should be lucky enough to have an agent like Laura Dail of the Laura Dail Agency and the sly intellect and insight of an editor like Sarah Hochman. Immense gratitude to Bill Maher for introducing me to David Rosenthal and the Blue Rider posse, including Aileen Boyle and Brian Ulicky. Thank you to Mary Ann Naples, Seale Ballenger and Zola Books.

Thank you to my tireless readers: Michelle Joyner, Maria Spiedel, Susan Norman, Ben Decter, Sascha Rothchild, Jillian Lauren and the brilliant Claudette Sutherland. S'loners: Sandra Tsing Loh, Nancy Rommelman, Erika Schickel, Amy Alkon and Samantha Dunn. Friends: Tonya Pinkins, Heather Winters, Annie Hamburger, Gia Palladino Wise, Christine Romeo, Judith Newman, Barbara Wright, Marla Englander, Lauren Frances, Heidi Levitt, Stephanie Black, Neil Weisberg, the late great Suzanne Krull and the members of the Four A.M. Club. Robin Shlien, for twenty-two years of friendship. Carina Chocana,

Acknowledgments

Erika Rothschild, Janelle Brown, Heather Havrilesky and the Suite 8 Writers Room. Cathleen Medwick and *More* magazine. Felicity Huffman and WhattheFlicka.com. Marilyn Freidman and Writing Pad, LA. AKA Talent, Glenn Rosenblum, Kaplan/Stahler, and Andrew Farber Law. Thank you to my parents for giving me so many stories to tell. Thank you and love to the home team, my husband, Jeff, and our son, Ezra Kahn.

About the Author

Annabelle Gurwitch is an actress and the author of *You Say Tomato, I Say Shut Up*, a self-hurt marital memoir cowritten with her husband, Jeff Kahn, now a theatrical play in its third national tour; and *Fired! Tales of the Canned, Canceled, Downsized, & Dismissed*. Her *Fired!* documentary premiered as a Showtime Comedy Special and played film festivals around the world. Gurwitch gained a loyal comedic following during her numerous years cohosting the cult favorite *Dinner & a Movie*; her acting credits include *Dexter, Boston Legal, Seinfeld, Melvin Goes to Dinner, The Shaggy Dog* and *Not Necessarily the News* on HBO. Most recently, she starred in the adaptation of Grace Paley's *A Coney Island Christmas* by Pulitzer Prize–winning playwright Donald Margulies at the Geffen Playhouse. Live appearances include the New York Comedy Festival, 92nd Street Y, Upright Citizens Brigade Theatre, and story salons in both New York and Los Angeles. She has served as a regular commentator on NPR and a humorist for TheNation.com. Her writing has appeared in *More, Marie Claire, Men's Health*, the *Los Angeles Times* and elsewhere. Gurwitch is a passionate environmentalist, a reluctant atheist, and lives with her husband and son in Los Angeles.